IT'S TIME TO MAKE IT HAPPEN ON EARTH

IT'S TIME TO MAKE IT HAPPEN ON EARTH

Applying
Spiritual Principles
to the Problems of a Material World

David J. Condon

TRANSFORMATION PUBLISHING
Wayne, New Jersey

Cover painting "Earth Changes" by Nanette Crist
© Nanette M.A. Crist 1991

It's Time to Make It Happen on Earth
Copyright © 1993 by David J. Condon

First printing 1993

Although the author and publisher have exhaustively researched all sources to ensure the accuracy and completeness of the information contained in this book, we assume no responsibility for errors, inaccuracies, omissions, or any inconsistency herein. Any slights of people or organizations are unintentional. Readers should use their own judgement or consult a holistic medical expert or their personal physicians for specific applications to their individual problems.

ISBN 0-9635561-4-2

LCCN 92-84075

Printed in the United States of America

TABLE OF CONTENTS

INTRODUCTION

A Summary of the Spiritual Principles Applied in this Book

Humanity is currently experiencing a time of great change. This is the beginning of the "New Age." It is the age of spirituality, when we become more aware of our complete selves, physical and non-physical, and more aware of our purpose for living. As we enter this age we are experiencing an acceleration of spiritual growth and development.

As human beings we choose to achieve certain aspects of spiritual growth through entering physical lifetimes on the Earth. In each lifetime we learn by experiencing the positive and negative consequences of our thoughts and actions. When our thoughts and actions are directed by love and concern our lives are abundant and we are richly rewarded. But when we allow them to be negative and destructive to others we suffer the consequences. This is the process through which we have chosen to learn and grow.

We are currently living in a world of deep social problems. The existence of these problems suggests that as a society we are not relating to ourselves and the rest of creation with love as the driving force. Greed, jealousy, envy, selfishness, prejudice and hate all result in the destruction of our society and environment. If there was only love in the world then there would be no social problems and we would be living in a Utopia. However, before this can be realized we have much more growing to do.

Psychologists say that alcoholics must reach a point in their lives where they hit "rock bottom." It is usually only then that they realize they have a problem and begin to improve themselves and accept the help of others. This is a common trait of humanity, and collectively we currently are very close to hitting a "rock bottom" on this planet. We have for so long denied that we are slowly being consumed by

1

our selfishness and greed, concerned with only material interests and ignorant of our divine heritage. Our physical existence on this planet is but a speck compared to the infinite spiritual world of which we are also a part. This spiritual world wishes to help lift us out of this sorrowful existence, but it cannot until we are willing to leave behind our selfish attitudes.

In this book you will read about the nature and purpose of humanity. You will read my views on how this knowledge can be readily applied to discover simple and obvious solutions to our social problems. The proposed solutions are generally my opinions and may not represent the thoughts of everyone who considers themselves spiritual. However I believe they provide a good starting point for improving our society by expanding our views of ourselves and our world.

The remaining portion of this introduction provides a background of some common spiritual teachings of the New Age. First it defines the New Age, and then it gives an overview of the many techniques of obtaining enlightenment and guidance. I have provided this information to give the reader some familiarity with these subjects before applying them in the following chapters.

What is the "New Age?"

By the "New Age" we refer to the astrological Age of Aquarius, which began in this century and will continue for 2160 years. There are twelve ages, each associated with a sign of the zodiac. The ages have a physical correspondence with the position of the sun on the first day of spring each year. The point that the sun crosses the equator on this day changes about fifty seconds of arc from year to year. This is due to the wobble of the earth on its axis. It takes 26,000 years for the precession of the equinox to make one complete cycle around the earth, and an age corresponds to one-twelfth of that cycle.

Each age is related to a particular aspect of the progression of development of humanity. The Age of Taurus began with Adam, and during this period humanity was concerned with learning about matter. The people of that time built many great temples and monuments. Abraham lived near the beginning of the Age of Aries, and this was the period of action and conflict, marked by many great wars. Jesus was born shortly after the beginning of the Age of Pisces. In this age humanity established its beliefs, and we learned the lessons of love and humility from God's example of love in the flesh.

Now, the Age of Aquarius is upon us. This is the age of social awareness and humanitarian concerns. This is the beginning of a time when each individual will become increasingly concerned with the feelings of others. It is the age of spirituality. Humanity has finally grown to the point where we can begin to comprehend all the lessons of Jesus and the other great masters. Our eyes are opening so that we can perceive not merely the literal meanings of the teachings, but the deeper underlying concepts as well.

The Aquarian Age is believed to have begun sometime in the 1960s, although the exact beginning is not known precisely. However, knowing the exact time the age began is not of utmost importance since the influences of one age gradually diminish as those of the next build.

In the early part of this century, the emergence of a great prophet, Edgar Cayce, heralded the beginning of a new period of spiritual concerns. Cayce was a remarkable psychic who, between 1902 and his death in 1945, gave more than 14,000 recorded and documented readings in Virginia Beach, Virginia. The readings gave spiritual insights and messages to individuals and groups to help them solve difficulties in their lives. Sixty-eight percent of the readings concerned physical and psychological ailments, giving healing advice to those who heard of him and sought his help. Cayce's approach to healing was a holistic one. It was predicated upon helping the body to heal itself while uncovering the underlying spiritual, mental, and emotional disharmony causing the condition. Although very effective, this was an approach that is still rare in medicine today. As many people followed his advice and became well, Cayce's fame grew. The readings today serve as a living legacy to Cayce's work, as they continue to help those who discover them.

Besides the physical readings, Edgar Cayce also gave special readings termed life readings, which were given to help individuals discover the purpose for their lives. During these readings the questioner was told about previous lifetimes that were influencing the present one. These readings revealed the lessons that needed to be learned by the individual through the experiences of this lifetime and others. Often these readings gave past life information that helped the person with relationships and possible career decisions.

Talk of previous lifetimes was certainly out of the ordinary in those days and these ideas were even startling to Cayce at first. Cayce was one of the first to introduce large numbers of westerners to subjects such as reincarnation, karma, and soul development. His readings also discussed more familiar subjects such as the bible, nature, and music, but always in a spiritually enlightening context. Readings were also given for groups of people interested in researching a particular subject. One such group was the Glad Helpers. They obtained readings that gave a remarkable and unique interpretation of the book of Revelations.

The readings are kept in a library in Virginia Beach by the Edgar Cayce Foundation, and are available for loan or purchase by mail. Since you may wish to do your own research of the Cayce readings, I have followed excerpts from the Cayce readings that appear in this book by a number in parenthesis that refers to the identification number of the reading.

A more recent catalyst for the growth of the New Age movement has been actress Shirley Maclaine, with her remarkable biographical accounts of her personal spiritual quest. The sheer bravery and confidence with which she faces detractors and skeptics is an example of her strong faith, and a great inspiration to New Agers. She is one of many spiritual teachers who have helped to bring increasing popularity and interest to the New Age movement.

The Stanford Research Institute estimates that five to ten percent of Americans currently consider themselves "New Agers." Being a New Ager essentially means engaging upon a search for the metaphysical (beyond physical) aspects of oneself and creation. Most New Agers share an interest or belief in psychic phenomena and a general need to find a deeper meaning and purpose for their life. Although not a religion, the New Age movement is grounded in a firm belief in the presence of God within all of creation. This differs with the popular western religions which preach of an external divine being. New Agers believe that they, and everyone else, are one with God.

The Channeling Phenomenon

Shirley Maclaine has done much to popularize the phenomenon known as channeling. Channeling is the method by which much New Age philosophy, including the Cayce readings, has been obtained. It is the process of receiving information from a source beyond one's conscious self. Channeling can take many different forms. Some channels hear voices, while others see images. Some must be in a sleep state, while others can be fully conscious.

The classical type of channeling is that in which the source of the information is an identifiable entity. Typically the source will describe itself as a discarnate entity, often with many human lifetimes on the physical plane. This type of channeling is commonly called mediumship. An example of this type of channel is Kevin Ryerson. Kevin channels several distinct entities with names like John of Zebedee, and Tom McPherson, although Kevin usually refers to them collectively just as "Spirit." Kevin Ryerson is popularly known as the channel through which Shirley Maclaine received most of her early spiritual guidance. Other famous classic channels are J. Z. Knight, channel for Ramtha, Jach Pursel, channel for Lazaris, and the late Jane Roberts, channel for Seth.

Another type of channeling is Higher Self channeling. In this type of channeling, the information is coming from one's own superconscious mind, or Higher Self. Higher Self channeling may tap into various sources of information, including the Higher Selves of other entities, master teachers, and angels.

Edgar Cayce was an example of a Higher Self channel. Although Cayce was channeling a part of his own self, he was not consciously aware of what was transpiring or being said. However, when giving a life reading for someone, Cayce was sometimes aware of entering a place known as the Hall of Records. These records are the Akashic Records, and upon them are recorded all thoughts, events, and actions. A channel such as Cayce can attune their consciousness to read all there is to know about any given individual from this infinite library of information. This includes not only the thoughts, events, and actions of this lifetime, but of all the lifetimes of an individual.

The Akashic Records are said to be in the domain of the Universal Mind. This is that primary spiritual substance from which all things have their beginning. It is what New Agers call God, but in this definition God is not an individual. Instead, God is the life force behind all that is. In this sense, God is the "Father" of everyone and everything.

Although Edgar Cayce left this plane decades ago, there are others alive today who serve as interpreters of the Universal Mind. The Aquarian Church of Universal Service is an organization devoted to maintaining a clear channel for this information. The Aquarian Church refers to this source as Cosmic Awareness. Cosmic Awareness is channeled by a few individuals who have been carefully trained to give accurate interpretations of what they "read" from the Universal Mind. Cosmic Awareness is the same source of information that was tapped by Edgar Cayce. It continues today to give helpful guidance to individuals, and to humanity as a whole.

Cosmic Awareness readings are published by Cosmic Awareness Communications (CAC) as a newsletter. Quotations from Cosmic Awareness readings are followed in this book by the number of the particular CAC newsletter in which they appear.

Back in the nineteenth century there lived another interpreter of the Universal Mind, and his name was Levi. Levi was the channel through which a book entitled *The Aquarian Gospel of Jesul the Christ* was received. This book is the interpretation of the specific Akashic Records that refer to the life and teachings of Jesus. Because of its source, it contains much more information than the New Testament. For instance, the bible mentions very little of Jesus as a youth and young man. However the Aquarian Gospel gives detailed records of the time that Jesus spent in Tibet, Egypt, India, Persia, and Greece. In these countries he studied the sacred teachings of their ancient cultures. It is my belief that this book is more accurate and complete than the New Testament, which was edited and rewritten to suit those in power during the early life of the Christian Church.

In the chapters that follow this introduction, there are many quotations from channeled material. For those readers who have trouble accepting information simply because it is channeled, let me suggest that you read in your own bible about the source of its information. For example, at the beginning of Revelations John says, *"I was in the Spirit on the Lord's Day, and heard behind me a great voice, as a trumpet. Saying, I am Alpha and Omega, the first and the last; and, what thou seest, write in a book . . .."* (Rev. 1:10-11) Ezekiel says, *"In the thirtieth year, in the fourth month, on the fifth day of the month, as I was among the exiles by the river Chebar, the heavens were opened, and I saw visions of God. On the fifth day of the month, the word of the Lord came to Ezekiel the priest . . .."* (Ezek. 1:1-3) I do not see any difference between these prophets of biblical time, and Edgar Cayce, or Levi, or the interpreters of Cosmic Awareness. They are all channels for the word of God.

On the other hand, I do not believe that just because something is channeled, it is true beyond question. This is because interpreters are still only human and can make mistakes like the rest of us. Also, when discarnate entities are channeled, we may not always be certain that they are much more knowledgeable than we. Consequently, Cosmic Awareness tells us to question everything. If something does not agree with and complement my ideals, I usually leave it alone for the time being. Although I must admit that this is rare, and more often than not I come back to this material in the future and I realize that it was not the information that was the problem, but it was I who was not ready to comprehend it.

Eastern versus Western Spirituality

Although the New Age movement is just beginning to catch on in the West, many of its teachings and principles are found in the very ancient religions of the East. For example, the belief in reincarnation is fundamental to both Hinduism and Buddhism. The ultimate importance of spiritual development and recognition of our oneness with God and everything that exists are also basic to these cultures.

While eastern culture has been spiritually oriented for many thousands of years, western society has been mostly material oriented. This is because the traditional focus of eastern culture has been to put aside material things, and escape into the knowledge of oneself in the higher spiritual realms. In contrast, western culture has concentrated on using and molding material form to suit physical needs. This is why most inventions and technological growth have occurred in the West. However, both approaches to life are necessary if we are to fulfill our purpose on Earth.

A good example of an eastern spiritual practice is that of yoga. Practitioners of certain yoga techniques attempt to attune their consciousness to experience a perfect state of spiritual enlightenment. This is known in Hindi as samadhi, and is the state of experiencing God in all things. A practitioner of yoga meditation attempts to dissociate from the world around them to discover the world within.

This dissociation from stressful worldly concerns is exemplified in the present culture of India. The material world traditionally has little significance to most Indians. As most Americans spend a minimun of eight hours a day at their job, Indians only spend an average of five. Whereas Americans receive an average of two weeks vacation per year, Indians receive more than a month. Indians value their leisure time and their time with their family much more than they value material comforts. That is why most Indians live in conditions most Americans would consider poverty. This is the fundamental difference in values between traditional eastern and western cultures.

In the West we place much greater emphasis on materiality. However, many New Agers have successfully incorporated eastern philosophies into their lives while living in a material-based culture. The result is a blending of spiritual and material emphasis, through which material creation is guided by spiritual attunement. Instead of divorcing ourselves completely from materiality, we attempt to bring God's kingdom to perfect manifestation on this material plane. We do this by first recognizing the perfection within and around ourselves, and then governing our mundane activities with this wisdom. Thus, we do not ignore our mundane life, but we try to illuminate it with divine wisdom. Unfortunately, most people in western society are ignorant of their spiritual nature and have not yet learned to integrate material living with divine purpose. This is the basis of all the problems we currently face.

Western people generally rely upon their church or religion for their spiritual expression. However, Christian religions are generally limited

IT'S TIME TO MAKE IT HAPPEN ON EARTH

to an exoteric interpretation of the bible. That is, they teach a literal translation that only skims the surface of the true underlying meaning. In the New Testament, Jesus often revealed these deeper meanings in parables. Jesus taught in parables so that only those who were ready to open their hearts to God could understand. Only those who are willing to forego their personal ambitions and gratifications are able to receive divine guidance. Jesus often prefaced his words with, *"He who hath ears to hear, let him hear."* This was his way of telling us to listen for the underlying esoteric (hidden) meaning. In the Piscean Age that Jesus lived, most people could not fully comprehend his words. However after Jesus ascended into heaven, the Holy Breath (Holy Spirit) came to continue our lessons. In this new age, the Holy Breath will open our minds so that now we can understand those things that were kept secret until this time.

When Jesus came into the earth at the beginning of the previous age, he did not bring a new religious doctrine. Instead, he illuminated the ancient Jewish teachings with deeper interpretation and application. Jesus tried to show the Jews that they had been too concerned with obeying the letter of their laws and teachings, and were not living the spirit of the laws. Today we still don't understand the significance of this difference.

Fortunately, the New Age is bringing further illumination to our religious doctrines. After each age we begin a new phase of spiritual evolution, and as we take this step we receive greater illumination and wisdom. We are similar to school children who, after successfully passing one grade level, move onto the next grade and receive greater learning and understanding.

But just as the Pharisees condemned the teachings of Jesus, many Christian leaders today condemn the New Age Movement. There will always be those who will resist change. They are threatened by new things because they are not secure with their own foundation. Those who are secure and have faith in themselves are not threatened by change. Clearly, the church is losing the respect of many people. As congregation memberships continue to shrink, people are finding that the Church is not providing the answers they seek. People are evolving and changing. If religion is to survive, it must change with them.

Through the man Jesus, God's love was manifested in the Christ. As the Christ, Jesus served as the pattern for us all to follow. This is what he meant by, *"I am the way."* Jesus showed us the potential and the ultimate destiny of humanity. At the end of his life on Earth, his carnal flesh was transformed to flesh divine. In other words, every atom of his body had become perfectly attuned with the will of the Father. As a man, Jesus was faced with all the trials and temptations

8

we all are. However, he showed us how to overcome these, and by doing so himself, he emblazoned the path for all of us to follow. Once he had achieved this in the resurrection, all power and glory were his. This laid the path for us all to take.

Our purpose on Earth is to overcome the problems created by the ego and carnal desires, and to attune them to the divine will. To enter the kingdom of heaven of which Jesus spoke, we must rid ourselves of all the baggage that has to do with self so that we can find and pass through the very narrow entrance into heaven and reunite ourselves with God. It is important to realize that this concept of heaven is not one of an actual physical place, but a state of consciousness that exists within each person.

A simple rule to live by to help us be more God-like in our dealings with everyday concerns is to ask ourselves, "How would Jesus respond in this situation?" Another question you can ask yourself is, "How should I react for the highest good of all concerned?" To become Christ-like in our relationships with others should be our life's primary objective. Otherwise we are destined to continue living the same problems repeatedly until we get it right.

Go Back and Try It Again—Reincarnation and Karma

The belief that our existence is much more than one physical lifetime, is fundamental to New Age philosophy. It is also widely accepted in nearly all eastern religions and cultures. Many, when they first hear the word "reincarnation," mistakenly believe that it refers to human beings coming back as animals or insects in their following lifetimes. This is generally not the case. Human spirits, with their divine gift of free will, would be too limited in the body of an animal which relies solely on instinct.

Reincarnation is the belief that the physical body is only a temporary housing for the soul while it is on the physical plane. It is the belief that the soul survives physical death and returns to the physical plane in another body when it is ready. Thus, the body is like a garment of clothing that the soul puts on temporarily, and then discards when it is finished with it. Later, the soul then creates a new body that is optimally suited for a new lifetime on Earth.

Most people live many lifetimes on Earth before they complete their soul development. However, after a lifetime on Earth, the soul may not necessarily reincarnate immediately on the Earth plane again. There are many other planes of existence where a soul may dwell. These planes are more like planes of thought than planes of matter. Sometimes a soul will choose to remain in spirit form to help someone else who is living on the physical plane. In this role, the soul is commonly called a spirit guide.

Karma is the law of cause and effect, and it is the basic principle that is responsible for our spiritual development. Karma is essentially the subconscious retention of all an entity does or thinks. It is responsible for bringing one's own will in accord with God's will. An entity who hurts another must suffer a similar act done to him so that the entity may realize the harm in what was done and repent. Often this comes in nearly identical form to the malicious act that was originally done by the entity. For instance, an entity who murders a person may be killed by that very same person in a following lifetime. This cycle may continue this way until one or both of the entities grow sufficiently to forgive the other person and themselves without taking retribution. This principle is clearly given in the bible as *". . . for whatsoever a man soweth, that shall he also reap."* (Galatians 6:7)

Reincarnation, on the other hand, is not as easily found in today's bible. That is why most westerners are slow to believe in the idea of multiple lifetimes. The reason reincarnation is scarcely found in the bible, is because a sixth century Byzantine emperor and his empress ordered all references to it deleted out of the bible.

Emperor Justinian (483-565) and his Empress Theodora together headed a diabolic dictatorship that murdered thousands of people in the name of Christ. They believed themselves to be far above ordinary people and answered any threat to their power with death. They saw the principle of reincarnation as a threat, because it meant that they would have to balance their karma as ruthless dictators in future lifetimes when they were no longer powerful. This teaching greatly disturbed Justinian and Theodora because they sincerely believed that they would become deities after they died and would retain their exalted status, never having to balance their karma. But the law of karma teaches that all souls must pay for their deeds, and through reincarnation, Justinian and Theodora would be made to live lives of atonement to balance all they had done. Thus, Justinian ordered the Fifth Ecumenical Congress of Constantinople in 553 A.D. to wipe all references to reincarnation out of the bible. The Pope of the time, Virgilius, was not permitted to take part in the Congress, and therefore had no part in approving the changes that were made. For more information on this time in history, read Noel Langley's book, *Edgar Cayce on Reincarnation.*

There are, however, a few passages in the bible indirectly referring to reincarnation that survived the massacre. For example, when Jesus

10

asked his disciples, *"Whom do men say that I, the Son of Man, am?"* they responded, *"Some say John the Baptist, others say Elijah, and others Jeremiah or one of the prophets."* (Matthew 16:13,14) Since the people mentioned by the disciples were all dead, there must have been a common belief in returning from the dead. In another passage, Jesus clearly says that John the Baptist was the reincarnation of the prophet Elijah, *"And as they went away, Jesus began to speak to the crowds concerning John: 'What did you go out into the wilderness to behold . . . a prophet? Yes, I tell you, and more than a prophet. This is he of whom it is written, 'Behold, I send my messenger before thy face, who shall prepare the way before thee.' Truly I say to you, among those born of women there has risen no one greater than John the Baptist . . ., and if you are willing to accept it, he is Elijah who is to come. He who has ears to hear, let him hear.'"* (Matthew 11:7-15)

Fortunately, *The Aquarian Gospel of Jesus the Christ* gives the words of Jesus as they were, and not as some people would have liked them to be. The following is one clear reference to reincarnation found in this book:

> And Jesus said, *"We cannot look upon a single span of life and judge of anything. There is a law that men must recognize: Result depends on cause. Men are not motes to float about within the air of one short life, and then be lost in nothingness. They are undying parts of the eternal whole that come and go, lo, many times into the air of earth and of the great beyond, just to unfold the God-like self."* (Aquarian Gospel 114:27-29)

The Tools of the Trade: Astrology, Numerology, Palmistry, The Tarot, The I Ching, and the Psychic Faculties

It is a tragedy that western culture has for so long remained close-minded to the existence of a spiritual self that predates physical birth and survives physical death. For once one believes that such a part of them exists, they can begin to find ways to contact it and receive guidance from it.

The conscious mind is limited in what it knows to the experiences of the current lifetime. The subconscious mind, however, remembers the experiences of all the entity's lifetimes. The superconcious mind, also called the Higher Self, is the entity's link with universal consciousness, and through it, all knowledge can be obtained. God does not wish for us to be cut off from Him, however our ego has led us away from His kingdom into the experiences of carnal life. Because we normally don't consciously remember anything before this life, we don't naturally accept the notion that we are anything more than our physical self.

There are, however, certain tools and techniques that we can use to discover the vast part of us that our conscious mind doesn't know. Some of these tools can help us to learn the unseen influences on our lives, while others can bring guidance from our Higher Self and provide answers to our everyday problems.

Astrology

Astrology is one technique by which a person can learn much about their own inner and outer qualitiies and their chosen life path. It can be thought of as the study of one's pre-natal choices for these qualities and their life experiences. Before we are born the soul seeks to construct a physical body and a personality that will provide the proper vehicle for these chosen experiences. The positions of the planets in the sky at the time of birth are said to symbolize these choices. Because we have lived many lives before this one, astrology can show the direction from which we came, and what skills and talents we are bringing into this life with us. Edgar Cayce believed that between lifetimes on Earth, the entity lives in realms of consciousness each associated with a particular planet of our solar system. He often used a person's birth chart to determine the influences an entity brings with them from these planetary sojourns.

When an astrologer prepares a birth chart for a client, they can decipher such things as a person's likelihood of succeeding in business, relationships with friend's and family, romantic relationships, possible career choices, and many other aspects of human life. Interestingly, my own birth chart suggests a strong love of metaphysical subjects.

Subtle vibrations of the planets influence us throughout our lives, serving as reminders of our chosen life experiences reflected in our birth chart. Everyday of our life one or more planet is positioned at an angle that stimulates a certain aspect of our birth chart. During the period of a particular planet's influence, we will be subconsciously swayed to feel and behave so that we confront a chosen life experience. To predict these influences, astrologers prepare progressed charts that compare the current positions of the planets with the positions in the birth chart. Progressed charts can then be used to prepare one for significant experiences such as a career change, a new romantic relationship or divorce, or an illness.

It is very important to note, however, that astrology can only indicate the tendencies of an individual. What course a person's life will take is up to them. For example, a person can choose to use their natural talents and abilities and develop them into a career, or they can choose to engage in other pursuits based upon monetary reasons or the desires of their family. Herein lies the importance of the study of astrology. Through astrology, one can quickly discover their own inner qualities and talents. Once a person knows these, they can use their will to accentuate and develop their positive traits and talents, while controlling their negative tendencies.

Numerology

Numerology is a companion study to astrology. Where astrology interprets the vibrations of planets, numerology interprets the vibrations of numbers. In numerology, the vibrations of the numbers contained in your birth date suggest the lessons you came into this life to learn. The letters in your name also are very significant in numerology. Each letter is assigned a numerical value, and the study of these vibrations reveals a person's inner attitudes and feelings, their outer personality, and their talents.

Numerology is also unique in that a person can change some vibrations they are experiencing. For example, if a person uses a name different from their birth name, and people begin to know them by that name, then different experiences and circumstances may occur in their life. These will be added to the influences of the birth name, perhaps greatly expanding one's experiences. When a woman gets married and changes her last name to that of her husband's, she is adding a new set of numbers to her original set. These new vibrations may alter the experiences she draws to herself.

To understand something about vibrations, imagine how you might think about a person whose name is Scott. Now imagine that Scott changes his name to Horatio. Doesn't this conjure up a completely different image in your mind? The vibrations of numbers also apply to the names of things, such as the name of a business or the title of a book. The name that one gives to something influences the type of success they are likely to experience with it. This is because the name determines the vibrations other people will feel when they hear it.

Palmistry

Palmistry is the study of the hands and the markings on them.

Palmists believe that the markings that appear on the hands indicate a person's personality characteristics, their inner needs and tendencies, and the overall direction of their life. The lines are similar to a road map that shows one's life path. Lines which appear in the hand are a result of nerves that end in the hand and are linked to the brain. Because of this connection to the brain, the lines may reveal a picture of what lies hidden in the subconscious mind of the individual.

A person's left hand is said to reveal the potentials that a person is born with, or what lies in the subconscious mind. The right hand indicates the qualities a person is using, or what lies in the conscious mind. However if you are left handed the reverse is true for you. By comparing the two hands, one can bring into awareness those talents and abilities that are commonly being utilized and those that are being neglected.

Palmistry is one tool that clearly reflects the action of the will to choose the direction of one's life. Over time, the lines on a person's hands change to reflect the new directions of their life. This shows that our future is not fixed, and we can change it by the choices we make in our lives.

The Tarot

The Tarot is a very effective technique to obtain guidance from a person's Higher Self. Tarot cards operate on the principle of symbology. Each of the exotic pictures on the cards contains several symbols that have an esoteric meaning associated with them. These symbols are similar to those that appear in dreams. However, most people can't understand their dreams or the cards because they don't know the language of symbols. Symbols are the language of the subconscious mind, and if one wishes to understand this part of themselves, they need to become familiar with this language.

The tarot cards are a representation of the many phases and aspects of human existence. The deck consists of a total of seventy-eight cards. The 22 cards of the major arcana symbolize the development of the soul in the different experiences a person encounters. Studying the major arcana cards and the symbols on them is often recommended as a path toward spiritual enlightenment. The 56 cards of the minor arcana deal more with the mundane concerns of everyday living, and the people who are an influence. A tarot reading consists of the client shuffling the cards, and then the cards being laid out in a certain pattern by the reader. The position each card takes in the layout determines the particular area of the person's life it is referring to with regard to the past, present, and future. It is believed that the person's Higher Self is controlling their hands when they are shuffling the cards, thus putting the cards into the proper order to convey the message. The tarot card reader then interprets the spread by analyzing the positions of the cards and recalling the meanings of the symbols on them.

In any method of divination, one can only reveal the future based upon the influences that are present at the time of the reading. In this way a reading can serve as a warning. If the person doesn't like what the tarot cards are telling them, they can use their will to change their destiny.

The I Ching

The I Ching, also known as The Book of Changes, is a very ancient book of Chinese wisdom. It is commonly used as a simple method of personal divination. Through an apparently random selection, the questioner is guided to read the chapter in the book that will best lead them. The chapter is selected by tossing coins or yarrow stalks. In the Chinese tradition fifty yarrow stalks are cast several times to arrive at a set of six numbers. These numbers are converted to a set of solid and broken lines called a hexagram. In the West it is more common and much simpler to toss a set of three coins six times to arrive at the numbers for the hexagram.

There are four types of lines in a hexagram, of which two of them are called changing lines. Two hexagrams are generated, one with the lines as originally cast, and one with the changing lines as their opposites. The first hexagram is said to represent the situation as it currently exists, and the second is what it will become. As the person is performing the casting of the stalks or tossing of the coins, they concentrate on a particular question they would like answered. In this system the Higher Self is guiding the person to cast the appropriate hexagram to convey the proper message. After the hexagrams are completed, the person looks up the appropriate interpretations in the Book of Changes.

There are also other simple forms of divination that a person can use to obtain guidance. Some more popular ones include the Book of Runes, tossing dice, and shuffling dominoes. In all systems of divination, one is relying on their own Higher Self to communicate with them through this device. Many people prefer to think of these tools in terms of synchronicity, which is a term coined by Carl Jung that means meaningful coincidence. Although these can all be very powerful tools, many people are able to use a more direct method. This is the use of their own psychic faculties and intuition.

IT'S TIME TO MAKE IT HAPPEN ON EARTH

Psychic Abilities

A surprising fact to some is that we all have the potential to be psychic. Some people, having developed these talents in previous lifetimes, are born with highly developed psychic skills. One such person was Edgar Cayce. But people of this type are rare. Most people in this lifetime have to develop psychic ability gradually, as their awareness of their spirituality progresses. Psychic abilities are a natural outgrowth of spiritual development. However, not all psychics are highly spiritual.

Psychic ability is a talent, much like playing the piano. Some people can learn to play the piano easily and become very accomplished at a young age, and others have to work harder at it. They must develop their talent over time. Talents are a result of past lifetimes during which certain abilities were developed and stored in the subconscious mind.

There are many different forms of psychic ability, but all are a direct result of breaking down the barrier that exists between the conscious self and the subconscious mind. Psychic abilities are a natural consequence of striving to attune oneself to God's will. Although, not all psychics are spiritual people. To reach and understand God's will one must open the door of the subconscious mind, for through this door God's voice is heard. Once one begins this process of attunement, then the mind and body begin to become a channel through which God may work. Many people hear the voice of their Higher Self speak to them, some see pictures or images, and others just experience an inner knowing.

There are several steps you can take to develop your own psychic faculties. The first is a very simple one: pay attention to your dreams. While asleep, your conscious mind becomes quiet and you become alert to your subconscious mind. Most dreams are just images of things that concern you in your everyday life and don't contain any extra information. However, in some dreams the Higher Self is sending you a message. These dreams are easily recognized by their often abstract symbolism, and seemingly nonsensical meaning. By studying the symbols in these dreams you can often reveal a very important message that has to do with your present or future.

A second step toward psychic guidance is meditation. Meditating regularly is the single most important activity a person can do to attune to the divine. During meditation one travels with their consciousness into the subconscious mind, seeking to know their inner self and hear the voice of God.

A final step is to have faith. One who has faith in themselves and in God can accomplish anything. Once one becomes attuned to the divine will of God, then all they need in their life is freely given to them. Remember that Jesus preached the power of faith and served as the model for us to follow.

The New Age movement is filled with lifetimes of information to study and learn. This introduction has only provided a glimpse of the tip of an iceberg. In the rest of this book I hope to show how this knowledge can be used to explain some problems of our society and our world, and how in moving toward increased spiritual awareness we can begin to solve them. This book focuses upon applying spiritual principles, for knowledge without application is like a sail without wind. As Edgar Cayce once said, **"It is not what one knows that counts, but what one does about that it knows!"** (1182-1)

CHAPTER ONE

Poverty

Everywhere we look in this world there are many people living in lack of the basic necessities of life. Even in a country as prosperous as the United States, an estimated 31.9 million people live below the poverty level. On television we see children and families in other countries who are literally dying from malnutrition. This is a sharp contrast to the lives most of us lead. Seeing those children often prompts us to ask ourselves, "How can those people be dying from hunger while most other people in the world have an abundance of food, and so many others are filthy rich?" Also, "Why does it have to be that way, and what can be done about it?" "What is the reason that those poor people are even here?" "Can people who constantly live in pain from malnutrition and are all consumed in just surviving, possibly be contemplating such things as their soul's purpose, spiritual development, and universal love?"

Who Suffers from Poverty?

I believe most people who suffer from poverty are of three general types. The first type I will call the karmic victim. This person is suffering from lack in this life because they probably chose to before coming into it. Between lifetimes on Earth we live consciously on other planes, and we choose our parents and environment before reentering the physical plane. This choice is based upon balancing the relationships we may have had in the past and optimizing our opportunity for soul growth. A person who chooses a poverty-stricken environment may be seeking to balance a previous lifetime of selfishness and greed. They could be seeking to learn to care about and have compassion for others more than they have cared about material possessions. Thus, they have chosen life experiences that give them opportunity to grow in this area.

The second type of person I will call the social victim. This person suffers from lack because of false conditioning by their parents and peers. They have been taught that because the rich are hoarding all the wealth, there are not enough resources left for everyone to have an abundance. This false belief is what keeps many unfulfilled and resenting others.

Finally, the third type of person I will call the sacrificial victim. This person, although probably not consciously aware of it, chose to be born into poverty and suffering so that society as a whole may benefit in coming together to give aid. I believe that this third type of person is prominent among the starving people we see on television.

Now let's return to the karmic victim. We are all governed by the Law of Karma, the law of cause and effect. As we live our many lifetimes on this planet what we do in each affects our fate in this life and the following ones. If we hurt someone in this lifetime, then they or someone else will likely hurt us back. If it's not in this lifetime, then it will be in another. That is, unless the person we hurt is wise and loving enough to forgive us without taking retribution, so that the karmic chain may be broken. However, the chain is not broken until we can forgive ourselves.

Our unkind acts are stored in our subconscious mind. How we feel about ourselves is directly related to how well we have been able to forgive ourselves for our past transgressions. Karma is healed this way through the Law of Grace. The Law of Grace is manifested by unselfish giving to others. Through works of kindness we are able to balance our misdeeds and forgive ourselves and one another. Cosmic Awareness describes the importance of forgiveness in the Law of Mercy:

> *The Law of Mercy is that Law which allows one to forgive all error—to forgive equally those who err against you, as you err against them. This is to be merciful. To be merciful is akin to the Law of Love, and if one obeys the Law of Mercy, there can be no error in the world.*

Karma is essentially the principle which urges us to achieve balance in our inner selves. Any unkind thought or action toward another creates an imbalance that must be corrected by an experience of opposite polarity. For example, if you steal from someone, then you must be stolen from. The only way to escape karma is through the Law of Grace. Forgive others, and then you will be forgiven. That is what we pray for when we say, "Forgive us our debts, as we forgive our debtors," in the Lord's Prayer. Give unselfishly to others, and forgive any who harm you. This is how you can release yourself from karma.

The karmic victim is like all of us who are bound by our actions. We are the victims of our own creations. Although, it often seems to our conscious mind that good and bad happen to us without deserving it. Many poor people may believe that they are just victims of bad luck. But there are many karmic reasons why a person may have chosen to live in poverty in a given lifetime. We have probably all experienced lifetimes of both severe poverty and extreme wealth, just so we could learn our individual lessons about materialism. Certainly one who belongs to the royal aristocracy and lives in a bastion of wealth, without concern for giving aid to the starving masses, will need to experience a role reversal in the future to balance the scales. Perhaps they will then gain the compassion and love for others less fortunate. This is most definitely a requirement before one may gain entrance to the kingdom of heaven.

On the other hand, the type of person I call the social victim is not tied karmically to being poor. However, they might have chosen a difficult environment to begin this life as a way of challenging themselves. A life of humble beginnings can often provide extra incentive to work harder and achieve great things. A person who is born rich and has everything handed to them may not possess this same motivation.

New Age teachings of the laws of abundance clearly state that it is within the power of everyone's Higher Self to create whatever it is they need. Perhaps this is one of the lessons that the social victim has chosen to learn by experiencing poverty and then discovering the way to prosperity through faith.

A technique we can use to achieve prosperity is to link our thoughts with our Higher Self, mentally visualize and "magnetize" what we want, and draw it to us. This technique applies the idea that our thoughts are things, and they are what shape our reality. If we can visualize ourselves as abundant and prosperous, then this will become our reality if it is in accord with our Higher Self and our chosen life's path. As Edgar Cayce once stated, ". . . **the Mind is the builder . . .**" (1472-2)

Unfortunately, the social victim is also affected by the thoughts of others around them. For one to magnetize money and objects and bring them to them, they must only have positive thoughts about those things and why they should have them. It is difficult to have only positive thoughts about anything, but especially so when others around you, such as your parents and peers, are negative about their own circumstances. Their negative thoughts reinforce your own fears and doubts. If you do not believe yourself worthy of prosperity, then you will block your own efforts to achieve it. This is why forgiving yourself for past mistakes is important. Also, you must want to see others prosperous, so that you do not harbor any guilt about your own wealth.

The Law of Prosperity is given by Cosmic Awareness as follows:

> *The Law of Prosperity states that one prospers in direct proportion to the enjoyment one receives in seeing the prosperity of oneself and others. And that one's prosperity is denied in direct proportion to one's own feeling of guilt for being prosperous, or at the envy and hostility one feels on witnessing others' prosperity.*

> *This Law states that when one prospers, all may prosper. The Law of Prosperity works for those who hold images, feelings, actions, dialogue and attitudes associated with beauty, joy, love and prosperity, and works against those who hold images, feelings, actions, dialogues and attitudes associated with ugliness, self-pity, complaints, envy and hostility toward oneself or any other person, group, race or class.*

> *Those who think, feel, act and speak of themselves as being poor and needy must spend three times the energy for the same prosperity received by those who think, feel, act, and speak of themselves as being wealthy and prosperous. An attitude that dwells in depression leads the way to physical, spiritual, mental, social and financial depression.*

> *Those who maintain prosperous attitudes, even in states of poverty, are foreign to such states and will not be allowed to remain out of place in those poverty situations, but will instead be deported to those prosperous states where such prosperous attitudes belong.*

The sacrificial victim is similar to the karmic victim in that they chose the way of poverty before entering this lifetime. However, the sacrificial victim is really not a victim, but is a highly developed soul serving as a martyr for raising the human consciousness. This type of person may be common among the starving people we see on television. With their plight publicized around the globe, people and countries come together to give aid. This process of giving to others in need has the power to transform all of humanity. Serving others heals us on an inner level and balances our negative karma.

At this time humanity has chosen for there to be suffering on this plane so that there is a desire and need to help others. It is only through service to others that we may complete our soul development. Cosmic Awareness has stated that at the time of our "passing over" that we call death, each of us must answer the question: How many have you served, and how well? The answer to this question is an indication of our level of spiritual development.

Sacrificial victims are living and dying in poverty for our benefit. Of course, they are probably not consciously aware that this is their soul's purpose. However, their Higher Self has chosen this experience as a way to serve others and in return gain greatly in spiritual development.

The sacrificial victim is not only present in Africa and other areas of common starvation, but in all classes of society. I'm sure many of you have pondered questions like: Why do little children have to die? Why do so many children get cancer? Why are others born physically or mentally handicapped? In some of these cases the main reason is that their suffering stimulates others into acts of immense caring and service. Before birth, these souls sense that their future parents need an experience that will help them to set aside their personal concerns and give selflessly to another. Thus, the sacrificial victims are born disabled, or they get sick, to create this opportunity for growth for their family and themselves.

Why Poverty Exists

We should remember that poverty exists for our benefit. All of life, whether we choose to call it positive or negative, is a perfect set of experiences designed to promote our soul's growth. Whatever experience we find ourselves in is perfect and correct for us at that point in our development. People who are living in lack are doing so because they probably belong to one of the three categories of victims described above.

Society cannot do much for the karmic victim except help that person to discover the reason for their suffering and then help them to change it. The Law of Karma will not release a person until they have completed their lesson. Even if we were able to take a homeless person, feed them, clothe them, and give them a place to live, this may not permanently end their suffering. If one has incurred a karmic debt, that debt must be paid according to the Law of Karma. Maybe all we have done for that person is delayed the completion of the payment of that debt to another time. However, a selfless act of giving to that person just may be enough to trigger similar acts of kindness on their part. If they serve others, then these acts of love will help to pay back their debt. Then our act of helping them would not have been wasted.

Unfortunately, many people feel that society has a debt it owes them, and they expect and even demand others to take care of them. Obliging this type of person does not help them. Instead, it only helps them to run away from their problems and avoid facing them. As already stated, you can't escape the Law of Karma. It will eventually catch up with you. When people realize this and accept it, it becomes less easy for them to commit further acts of unkindness, knowing that like begets like. These people must learn to stop blaming others and accept that they are the cause and the creators of all their problems.

Our current system of welfare in this country often gives handouts to people without asking for anything in return. Although this seems a loving and unselfish gesture, it unfortunately does not adequately encourage the recipients to improve themselves. Instead, it gives them the message that the government and the people of this nation realize that they cannot survive on their own because they are somehow incompetent. This message must be changed. It can be changed by simply asking that the persons receiving welfare perform some community service in return. Soon after they begin to start giving instead of only receiving, they will realize their own self worth and value. They will see that what they do can be important and that they are important individuals. For many, this attitude alone can be the healing power for their life. It must be realized that to receive one must first give. One must put out to get back. One who does not contribute to others and society will never receive.

If a person is willing to give more, to work harder, then they should be able to receive more. This provides the opportunity and the encouragement for people to move out of their impoverished condition if they truly want to. Awareness points out that this is a major weakness in our present system. **"The problems with much of the welfare system today is that if entities make an effort to get a job when on welfare, they are punished and have their welfare taken away from them for any money they earn, or for going to school, or for doing anything to better their position."** (CAC 90-1) We are not encouraging them to improve themselves if, when they begin to try, we remove our assistance. If we are to serve the poor we must stop encouraging them to remain poor and stop treating them like outcasts of society. We should give all we can to the needy, but we should not be afraid to ask that they also contribute to their own welfare and to the welfare of the community. In doing so we will be affirming our belief in them.

Creating Your Own Abundance

Once a person recognizes that they are important and begin making contributions to society, they will be practicing the laws of abundance. These laws teach that everyone has the power to create their own abundance and there are enough resources available for everyone on the planet to have an abundance.

The laws of abundance are important for everyone to learn, not only the poor, but anyone who feels stuck or dissatisfied with their life. True abundance is having all one needs to do their life work, and it is natural for us to have these things. Creating abundance for yourself benefits the whole of society since each individual's life work is an important contribution to everyone.

Unfortunately, many people do not believe abundance is possible for them. They believe that others are hoarding all the riches of the planet, and there are none left for them. Ironically, it is these very beliefs that are forming their reality. Operating under the laws of abundance requires one to realize that mere thoughts may be manifested in material things. As Edgar Cayce said, " . . . **thoughts are things!**" (386-2)

The basic principle behind the laws of abundance is faith. They teach that by putting your faith in God and surrendering your will to Him, all of your needs will be met. Dr. Jon Speller, in his book *Seed Money In Action*, describes what he calls the Law of Tenfold Return. With this technique, you give a certain amount of money to a worthy cause as a seed. Then you imagine this amount of money returning to you multiplied by a factor of ten. By doing this with total faith, you reap your reward. By continuing this process repeatedly, you will be establishing a positive energy flow that will benefit all involved.

As an example, the following anecdote illustrates this power of faith. It comes from the autobiography of one of India's most famous yogis, Paramahansa Yogananda. As a boy, Paramahansa Yogananda already possessed the faith to operate under the laws of abundance. On a challenge from his older brother, Yogananda and a friend embarked on a journey to a nearby city without a single rupee (Indian money) between them. Leaving in the morning aboard a train, they were to return before midnight, without missing any meals, and without begging or telling their quest to anyone. Following all the rules of this "penniless test," Yogananda and his friend were greeted with open arms by strangers. They were fed, entertained, and given money for their return trip. When they returned and related their experience, his skeptic brother became convinced of the power of faith.

Jesus taught us this principle two thousand years ago, yet most of us are still not putting it into practice. Jesus said,

> *Therefore I tell you, do not be anxious about your life, what you shall eat or what you shall drink, nor about your body, what you shall put on. Is not life more than food, and the body more than clothing? Look at the birds of the air: they neither sow nor reap nor gather into barns, and yet your heavenly Father feeds them. Are you not of more value than they? And which of you by being anxious can add one cubit to his span of life? And why are you anxious about clothing? Consider the lilies of the field, how they grow; they neither toil nor spin; yet I tell you, even Solomon in all his glory was not arrayed like one of these. But if God so clothes the grass of the field, which today is alive and tomorrow is thrown into the oven, will he not much more clothe you, O men of little faith? Therefore do not be anxious, saying, "What shall we eat?" or "What shall we drink?" or "What shall we wear?" For the Gentiles seek all these things; and your heavenly Father knows that you need them all. But seek first his kingdom and his righteousness, and all these things shall be yours as well. Therefore do not be anxious about tomorrow, for tomorrow will be anxious for itself. Let the day's own trouble be sufficient for the day.* (Matt. 6:25- 34)

When Jesus fed five thousand people with only a few loaves of bread and fish, it was symbolic of God feeding all those with faith. Unfortunately, most of us do not possess this level of faith. We have been conditioned by our parents and others in our environment that such things are not possible. Remember Jesus said we must become like children if we are to enter the kingdom of heaven. Children have faith because they have not yet been taught their limits and doubts. Faith is natural for us. Doubts must be learned. Doubts block the natural flow of energy, and they prevent us from having all we need. If we can learn to have faith and release our doubts, then we will prosper. As Edgar Cayce stated, **"For what ye ask in His name, believing, and thyself living, ye have already."** (3049-1)

Becoming Aware of Your Life's Purpose

The most important thing for all of us is to try to become aware of our life's purpose. We need to be in touch with ourselves and our life work to realize our true value and worth. This helps us feel deserving of whatever we need. Why are we here? What should our life's work be? The answers to these questions come more naturally for most people than they realize. Usually the things you are good at and the ones that bring you the most satisfaction are what your life's work should be.

Amazingly, so many of us do not pursue the things that bring us the most joy. We have been led to believe that they are not practical or that they don't pay well enough. The happiest people in this world are the ones who are doing what they love and making a living at it. These people are following the guidance of their Higher Self, and their Higher Self brings them all that is needed for them. By not developing and using their natural talents, they make success more difficult to achieve.

People who pursue a career that does not utilize their natural abilities generally are not very successful at their job. Ironically, the Higher Self may try to free them from this situation by getting them fired or laid off. Many of the great and successful entrepreneurs of our time were fired from their last job. This event, which seemed tragic at the time, became the blessing of a lifetime for them.

Many people envy the rich and try to emulate them and become like them. It is time these people realize that many very wealthy people are not happy souls. Strong attachments to material things only eventually lead to disappointment. As humans we are not only physical beings. Our physical bodies are only a small portion of our makeup. Material riches can only satisfy us on the material level. This leaves our emotional, mental, and spiritual selves still unfulfilled. People who are caught up in making money usually give very little energy to these other parts of themselves, and are never really happy in their lives. Money can't buy love, nor can it buy intellect. Most importantly, money can't help buy one into meeting God. As Jesus said, *". . . it is easier for a camel to go through the eye of a needle than for a rich man to enter the kingdom of God . . .."* (Luke 18:25)

As I stated earlier, whatever situation a person finds themselves in, whether they are poor or rich, it is so they can learn an important lesson. Therefore, don't envy the rich and worship money the way they do, or else you also will have to learn the great disappointment and the great lie that money can buy happiness.

The tools of the trade mentioned in the introduction of this book can be of great help in learning the specific purposes your soul has in this lifetime. Astrology and numerology are both very easy ways to begin getting in touch with the reason you were born at the time you were and into the environment you chose. A reading with a skilled psychic also can be a great help in bringing your purpose into focus. Your Higher Self has all the answers you seek, and the tools of the trade can be effectively used to tap this wisdom.

Although becoming aware of our life's purpose is very important, we must not forget that we all possess an even higher spiritual ideal that is the common purpose for all our lifetimes. This ideal is to perfect ourselves and become again one with God as Jesus did. The way to perfect ourselves is through service to others. Give unselfishly to others; even when you yourself have very little. The rewards you obtain on the spiritual level are far greater than anything physical. Remember not to be selfish with what you do have. For, in His own words, ". . . man cannot lay treasures up in heaven and earth at once." (Aquarian Gospel 99:16) These are the principles that must be taught to the many who are unnecessarily suffering in this lifetime. These are the principles that have the power to set one free.

The Importance of Free Will

Proper use of these principles requires one to exercise their free will. A person's actions must be directed by proper use of their inner strength. We all must use our free will to make choices that will lead us down the path to prosperity for ourselves and everyone else. However, many people, such as those in African and communist countries, are oppressed and are denied the right to exercise their free will. Instead, their will is subjugated by the will of the government. Also, because these people have been treated so poorly by their government they lack faith in themselves and do not feel deserving of prosperity. Without the freedom to choose and make decisions for themselves, they have lost control of their lives and cannot properly use the laws of abundance.

For the resources to flow properly and the economies to improve in these places, human dignity must first be restored to the people. Only when there is freedom and openness will people begin to trust in themselves and others. Then each person is free to do their life's work, and they all share in the abundance of their land. Oppressive communist governments and dictatorships can never lead prosperous countries. When individual freedoms are taken away there cannot be prosperity, and the whole nation is doomed to economic failure.

Prayer for Prosperity

Dear Lord, we thank you for the blessings you have given us. We thank you for the power to choose our path and to learn and grow through our chosen experiences. Father, grant us whatever we need to fulfill our mission on this plane, and help us to know our purpose. May your will always be done in and through us, and may we always have faith in our ability to maintain favor in your eyes. Grant us the power to forgive others and ourselves when we do not act in harmony with one another and yourcreations. Your will be done Lord. Amen.

Meditation for Prosperity

Envision yourself in a lush garden of green plants and colorful flowers. Picture that you have with you your most prized creations. These may be some art or literature, or some photographs you've taken, or anything that represents something you have created that makes you most proud. Maybe you only have something abstract, such as an idea you once had. Imagine that you carried through on this idea, and now you have something with you in the garden that represents this. Now envision other people in the garden with you. Your friends and relatives are there, and also many people you don't know. These people are all coming up to you and admiring your creations. They are recognizing your talents and abilities as very special. Finally, imagine that they are giving you whatever you feel you most need or want, in exchange for being able to benefit in some way from your work. Recognize the satisfaction in knowing that you have made someone else's life easier or more joyful with your creations. Recognize how good you feel about receiving gifts from others. Stay in this place as long as you feel you want to, and know that you never have to leave it again.

CHAPTER TWO

Drug Abuse

The drug abuse problem is a social disease that is threatening virtually every element of society. Drug abuse is prevalent in our schools, our businesses, and our government. It is strongly linked to crime and blamed for many transportation accidents. Drug abuse is common among people of all ages, including young children. Among students, a recent poll reported that one in every five high school seniors admitted to using illegal drugs in the past thirty days. Among older people, one in five Americans between the ages twenty and forty are regular users of illegal drugs.

Drugs and Spiritual Awakening

As a part time musician I come into contact with many people who are users of illegal drugs. One of my closest musician friends has even invited me to try hallucinogenic mushrooms. He calls them "mind expanding" and "spiritually enlightening." This may easily be a temptation for someone like me who places strong emphasis on spiritual growth. However, I have learned that spiritual progress best occurs naturally. I am also aware of the pitfalls in rushing one's spiritual development artificially, although I do believe in using whatever natural tools are available. Some of these safe methods are meditation, prayer, crystals, and self-hypnosis.

For some people, hallucinogens probably do have an impact upon their spiritual awareness. They were commonly used by American Indians in their ceremonies and spiritual rituals. For them it was a tool to expand their awareness. But the indians recognized the responsibilities and risks associated with this ritual, and the medicine man carefully supervised the use of the drug. The drug most commonly used by indians is a cactus derivative known as peyote. In some places members of the Native American Church of North America possess the legal right to use this drug in their ceremonies. However, using drugs is a risky business. In Henry Leo Bolduc's book, The Journey Within, the Eternals, channeled by Daniel Clay Pugh, give this warning about the use of drugs for increasing one's spiritual awareness:

> There are those people who would try to short-circuit this by taking drugs that would open the consciousness. In effect, this creates what would be called "Pandora's Box." By so doing, you open an awareness which you are not able to accept. You open a reality which you are not prepared for physically, mentally, or spiritually, and which, in essence, could turn upon you and destroy you. But yet, if you prepare yourself, and are ready, then no matter what method you use to open the door, then you shall proceed and learn as you would or come to know and accept.

I believe that anyone who thinks they are spiritually ready to use drugs, or any other artificial technique of enlightenment, is mistaken. There are many psychological and physical changes that must occur during the spiritual growth process. These occur naturally under direction of your Higher Self. If you seek to rush your growth, you may not be able to handle the sudden changes.

In Shirley Maclaine's book, *It's All in the Playing*, Shirley explains the side effects she experienced when she used acupuncture as a quicker path to enlightenment. After rushing her own conscious expansion with acupuncture, Shirley became plagued by chronic sleeping problems. Since Shirley was already advancing rapidly in her spiritual development before she underwent the treatment, her side effects were not severe. However, the energy flow in her body was altered by the experience. A spiritual entity named Ambres explained to her during channeling through Sturé Johansson, that her problem stemmed from overstimulated superconscious energy. During sleep, the body's energy frequency changes as the superconscious mind supplants the conscious mind. Because of the overstimulation of the higher energies, an even frequency for the sleep state could not be achieved.

There are many things that seem a mystery to our conscious minds. I've heard many people, including preachers, say that as mere humans we are incapable of understanding God's purpose and the reasons behind many things that happen to us. I totally disagree with that thinking because I feel it underestimates the human potential. People who study the New Age teachings believe that our purpose as human beings is to increase our spiritual development, and upon completion of that development, become individual God beings at one with God's will. As God, there is no knowledge beyond our grasp. Jesus is our model. All He is, so can we become.

However, the expansion of our knowledge must be accompanied by an increase in our inner wisdom. The two must grow slowly together so that we are able to safely assimilate all we learn. Our Higher Self makes certain that each lesson is experienced at its proper time.

Humanity as a whole has been prevented from knowing much of the knowledge of the universe until we are ready. We have been protected from outside influences before we were ready to experience them. Thus we have been allowed to work privately on the group karma of the human race without interference. This is explained in the following discourse by the spiritual entity known as St. Germaine, channeled by Bob Fickes:

> We are now entering into a decade of very rapid transformation. Your Earth has been preserved in order that it might realign itself with all of the forces of nature or that which you would call God in this universe. It can also be said that your Earth has been protected.

> There were veils placed around Earth at the time of Atlantis to [prevent] any knowledge beyond Earth coming to Earth. This would include the knowledge of living beings beyond Earth's atmosphere. All of this was so that the Earth would be in a controlled environment for the final few thousand years prior to its transcendence.

> Earth was, in a manner of speaking, in a therapy session to heal its past, to bring to the surface the unresolved issues, and to work them through. It may be seen as an explanation for the past 6,000 years of your Earth's history, for there can be no other explanation for that which is seen truly as insanity.

We are given knowledge only when we are ready to receive it. It is often said, "When the student is ready, the teacher appears." This statement is generally applied to finding a spiritual teacher or guru, but it is just as applicable to listening to the teacher within. It is God's will that we all eventually share in the knowledge of the universe. But He only reveals it to us a piece at a time as we become more attuned to His divine will. Drugs artificially break down the barriers that protect us from experiencing more than we are ready to perceive. This makes them not only potentially physically, emotionally, and mentally damaging, but spiritually as well.

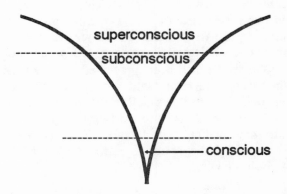

Cayce's Model of the Human Consciousness

The Human Mind

The human mind consists of three basic elements: the conscious mind, the subconscious mind, and the superconscious mind. Our connection with God and universal knowledge is through the superconscious mind, also known as the Higher Self. Spiritual guidance comes to our conscious mind from our Higher Self through our subconscious mind. In crossing the barriers of the mind and passing through the subconscious, the information may become distorted.

The pathway for guidance is like a pipe. If the pipe is loaded with debris, then fluid cannot freely flow through it. Your conscious mind is like a radio or TV tuner. You can adjust the frequency of your mind to receive a certain channel that carries the information you seek, but only if the air is free of static interference. Only through proper attunement can one provide a clear channel for guidance to reach the conscious mind. This attunement is gradually developed through prayer, meditation, and an earnest desire to tune in to one's Higher Self. It cannot be rushed artificially, for the pipe is not yet cleared of debris, and the mind cannot yet be selective to receive what it seeks.

The introduction of drugs into the body causes the synapses of the brain to short-circuit and the natural barriers of the subconscious to be crossed. The thoughts and emotions we experience, we may not be ready to perceive. Physical, emotional, mental, and spirtual side effects may result. Without the proper preparation we receive distortions and we lose control of the experience. This is quite different from when we receive this information through meditation. For during meditation the conscious mind always remains in control and we only receive as much as we are prepared for.

The subconscious is a storehouse for memories of our experiences. Often we bury emotions from painful or tragic events there, rather than face them all at once. In time we must face these emotions, learn their lessons, and forgive those who have hurt us. However, drugs can cause a sudden release of these memories and feelings, and an explosion of these emotions into our conscious mind can be too much for us to handle. Also, since the information is taking an unnatural path, it is being distorted. The combination of a sudden opening to the subconscious and the distortion of the information can cause what is commonly known as a "bad trip."

Once the barriers in our mind have been breached through the use of drugs it becomes easier for them to be crossed again without our control. This is what psychologists call "flashbacks." These disturbing experiences may occur weeks or even months after the drug has left the body. Flashbacks are illusions or hallucinations that may occur at any time and without one's control. To me, the possibility of side effects such as flashbacks and bad trips are strong deterrents from using hallucinogenic drugs.

Drugs as an Escape

I suppose most people who use drugs are not consciously seeking spiritual enlightenment, but just an escape from the burdens of everyday living. Currently non-hallucinogenic drugs, such as cocaine, are the most popular. People sometimes take these drugs because they believe the drugs help them to cope with the problems and pressures in their life, often using them as a crutch to lean on to help them keep going. The danger is that they gradually become dependent upon them psychologically and physically, causing damage to the mind and the body.

In today's society most people are living under tremendous pressure from responsibilities on their job, at home, or in relationships.

Sometimes unexpected tragedies, such as the loss of a loved one or loss of a job, result in people turning to drugs or alcohol to forget their sorrows. Their fear of experiencing and expressing their emotions results in their avoiding these feelings through substance abuse. Drugs seem to promise a temporary escape from the "real" world into a different one. Some people are just so frustrated with their life that they search for a way out. Soon the drug user realizes that these escapes are only temporary, and when the drug wears off they are returned to face their troubles. Tragically, many people try to make the escape more permanent by using the drugs more often and maintaining an almost constant high.

The piece of life's puzzle that these people are missing is the real reason for sorrows, or what I call prefer to call challenges, in a person's life. A fundamental principle in New Age philosophy is that every event in a person's life occurs for a reason and by their own soul's choice. Although unaware of it, each person's life is truly guided by their Higher Self. Before we are born we choose our parents and the environment into which we begin our life. We have a definite plan and direction for our life before we begin it. This plan, developed by our Higher Self, is always for our highest good and maximum spiritual development. Usually this plan involves working to resolve karmic debts incurred in previous lifetimes and to experience new situations for optimum soul growth.

However, drugs can prevent us from working out the karma we have chosen in this life. When under their influence we no longer act like ourselves. We gradually lose control of our personal will as the drug takes over. Our personality begins to change as aspects of the subconscious begin to emerge without control. Thus, drugs are a block to your spiritual growth. They interfere with your ability to direct your life and exercise your free will to fulfill your life purpose.

Perhaps even more frightening is the very real possibility of possession by an unwelcome discarnate entity. By relinquishing your self control and weakening your energy by taking drugs, you can be opening yourself up to another spirit who temporarily assumes control of your body.

How Drugs Open One Up To Possession

Unfortunately, many people who become psychologically addicted to drugs or alcohol, carry this addiction with them into the spirit world after they die. However on that level they cannot directly satisfy their obsession. Instead, many spirits of addicts tend to hang around living people who indulge in the same kind of substance abuse as their addiction. They attempt to attune themselves to the energies of people who are drinking or using drugs, trying to share their experience. Cosmic Awareness described the process in alcoholics in the following excerpt:

> **This Awareness indicates that they [spirits with addictions] attach themselves to the aura of an individual and assist in creating holes in the aura, whereby they can then siphon off some of the feeling and experience of the drinker; in this manner they vicariously experience the drinking of another so that they share in the indulgence. For the drinker, this entity will feel himself at times lacking control of himself and may experience expressions that are not characteristic of himself if he were not drinking. (CAC 90-14)**

The aura is the energy field surrounding a person that contains the higher level bodies. These bodies are the etheric, the astral, the mental, and the spiritual bodies. Each body surrounding a person contains and holds a portion of that person's non-physical self. The etheric body contains and holds the life force energy that a person uses for their own vitality. The astral body contains and holds one's emotional projections. The mental body holds the thoughts of the individual. And the spiritual body holds the Higher Self, or one's connection with God.

These bodies are less dense and more fluidic than the physical body, making them easier to penetrate. Under normal conditions a person's own will is strong enough to keep spiritual entities from penetrating their aura. However, drugs and alcohol have a weakening effect on the aura and make a person more susceptible to the deviant behavior of entities with a severe addiction.

Actual possession of a person's physical body can occur when their abuse becomes so great that they are weakened to the point that they cannot fight off the entity. Often, alcoholics and drug addicts have a need to escape from their own life. This lack of will to hold on to their life opens the door for another entity to take control.

The way for anyone to protect themselves from possession is to avoid abusing drugs and alcohol and to love themselves and love being who they are. Negative thoughts and emotions greatly weaken our energies. But if we maintain positive attitudes about ourselves and life, no hungry evil spirits can penetrate our aura. Jesus explained this in the following teaching he gave to a man from whom he had just removed an evil spirit:

> *If you will keep your mind fully occupied with good, the evil spirits cannot find a place to stay; They only come to empty heads and hearts. Go on your way and sin no more.* (Aquarian Gospel 89:20-1)

Contacting Your Higher Self

When born into this plane you are consciously separated from your Higher Self and you forget the intended purpose for this lifetime. Fortunately, your Higher Self attempts to send you subtle reminders to keep you on your chosen path. If we can learn to listen to our Higher Self we can obtain a deep understanding of our life plan and purpose. Through hearing the inner voice of our Higher Self we can pass through our lessons more quickly and achieve rapid spiritual growth. Thus, it is very important for everyone to find ways to contact and listen to the guidance of their Higher Self.

There are many ways our Higher Self attempts to speak to us and guide us. The easiest method for contacting your Higher Self is to pay attention to your dreams. Psychologists know from research that each of us dreams every night. During sleep, our busy, cluttered, conscious mind takes a rest and the subconscious takes over. In this state you are one step closer to your Higher Self, and often messages come through loud and clear. The only thing you have to do is to remember these dreams after you awake so that you can interpret them and put their guidance into use. You can do this by keeping a pad and pen near your bedside, and writing down each dream immediately after it occurs. You also can program yourself to wake up briefly after each dream by repeating in your head a phrase like, "I will awaken after each dream tonight," or "I will remember my dreams," as you are falling asleep.

Once you begin recording your dreams you will need to interpret the messages contained in them. Some dreams will carry a meaning that will be instantly clear to you. Others will be loaded with symbolism that you may not understand. Psychologists have studied dreams for many years and have found that many symbols in our dreams we share in common with others. Through research, they have been able to associate definite meanings with each symbol. For instance, to dream of falling usually represents some fear or insecurity in the dreamer's life, such as fear of losing their job or feelings of sexual inadequacy. A dream dictionary, available at your local bookstore, can sometimes be a useful tool in dream interpretation. A dream dictionary usually contains thousands of common symbols and meanings. You may want to buy two different ones and compare their meanings, because often there are several possible interpretations. Use your intuition to guide you to the proper meaning.

However, often the symbols in your dreams have personal meanings, and the dream dictionary may not contain that symbol or else its meaning won't seem right to you. For example, I have been told that when we dream about people we know, about eighty percent of the time we are not dreaming about them, but about what they represent to us. Often this is some characteristic of our own self that we associate with them. For example, my father appearing in a dream often to me means skepticism, or that part of me that is limiting my growth because of self doubt. Try meditating on these personal symbols when they occur to find the meaning they have for you.

Once you begin remembering your dreams, you will be open to a new world inside yourself. Occasionally, you may even have a truly profound experience known as a lucid dream. Lucid dreams are dreams you have that are usually so vivid that they are virtually indistinguishable from reality. In these dreams, however, you become aware that you are dreaming, yet the dream continues. Some how your conscious mind has gotten involved in the dream, and you can now begin to control it. Often, I'll be having a dream and I'll suddenly pause and say to myself, "Hey this must be a dream." However I'm usually not certain until I perform a test. What I like to do is create something, such as an apple, out of thin air simply by thinking about it. When it appears, I know that I'm in a dream, and then the fun starts. Lucid dreaming is a remarkable experience, and the best part of it all is that it's drug free. Lucid dreams are also a great way to confront and improve circumstances in one's life, since these situations can be acted out in one's dreams and various ways of dealing with them can be explored.

Lucid dreaming is sometimes similar to perhaps the best method of contacting your Higher Self: meditation. While meditating, a person attempts to quiet their thoughts and set aside their concerns, allowing their Higher Self to come into their awareness. Sometimes one experiences dream-like visions during meditation, or they see colors or hear voices. However, most people just gradually become aware of their inner self and they experience great clarity in their thoughts. In this state of altered consciousness the Higher Self is able to make one's purpose clear, and they are totally at peace. Meditation opens a direct channel to God. But the key is first to obtain stillness. To obtain guidance from your Higher Self, the mundane concerns of your life and relationships must be temporarily placed aside. As Jesus said, *"God's meeting place with man is in the heart, and in a still small voice he speaks; and he who hears is still."* (Aquarian Gospel 26:7)

Meditation, like dreaming, is something you probably already do without realizing it. For instance, whenever you are thinking intently about something you are going into the beginning stages of meditation. Focusing the mind on a particular thing, such as one's own breath, is a common technique for removing the cluttered, random thoughts that usually occupy the conscious mind. Perhaps when working hard, and concentrating intently about something, you may have sudden flashes of insight about what you were thinking or maybe about something totally unrelated. This is an indication that the doorway to your Higher Self has been opened through the power of concentration.

A good time to meditate is first thing in the morning, because the day has yet to begin and you probably have fewer thoughts or concerns to contend with. I usually find that many of my best and most creative ideas come to me first thing in the morning.

Another method of reaching the Higher Self is to begin paying closer attention to the events that occur during the daytime. Nearly every minute of every day we make a decision that influences the direction of our life. When making these decisions, we can generally choose from three possibilities. We can choose to listen to the mental conditioning of our parents and friends, living the life they think we should live; we can choose to do exactly the opposite because we resent their interference; or we can listen to our inner voice and do what feels right to us inside.

It is most important to remember that every event in our life has a purpose to it. Our Higher Self is guiding us to experiences that will present the best learning opportunities. Often we experience a series of "coincidences" that are more than just chance. These events may be an example of our Higher Self trying to communicate with us. Carl Jung called these meaningful coincidences "synchronicity."

During the writing of this book I have personally experienced many synchronistic events. It seems whenever I begin writing about a new topic, I am flooded with a barrage of information directly related to what I am trying to communicate. For example, earlier in this chapter I quoted from the entity St. Germain. I was prompted to turn to his teaching only after three separate events occurred very closely together. The first time I was introduced to St. Germain I was reading a book entitled *Star Signs* by Linda Goodman. She very briefly mentions his name as an example of a modern day spiritual guide who has lived many important earthly lives, including that of Shakespeare, Sir Isaac Newton, and Sir Francis Bacon. After I read this part of the book I continued reading on and had almost forgotten about him. Then I received in the mail my first issue of *Connecting Link* magazine. The first article I turned to was a channeled discourse on America by St. Germain. Although I found it interesting, it wasn't until the third event on the next day that I decided I would quote from this article. On that day I went to a friend's home and met a very learned gentleman named Bill, who to my astonishment began talking about this very entity named St. Germain. He had a very keen interest in this entity and seemed to know everything about him. This unprovoked discourse from my new acquaintance prompted me to give the magazine article a second look. It was then that I realized it carried an important message that related to my subject matter.

By paying closer attention to the events in your everyday life you should begin to notice synchronistic events that have an important message for you. This is especially true when you are consciously tuning in to receive guidance in this way. Once your Higher Self knows that you have chosen to communicate with it through dreams, meditation, or synchronicity, it will begin to make greater use of these avenues. Your Higher Self is constantly trying to reach your consciousness, and once a doorway is opened to it, you can expect much to come through.

In mentioning dreams, meditation, and synchronicity, I am giving the reader some safe and natural methods of psychic exploration. In most people, the unfoldment of psychic experience occurs gradually and only with persistent effort. Although drugs may be a short cut to these experiences, I doubt that someone under the influence could make sense of it. Besides, as I've already pointed out, the risks involved are unacceptable. The natural methods I've described are much more compatible with our physical and mental beings and are much more fulfilling to us in the end.

Of course, most people who take drugs are not conscious of attempting to achieve spiritual growth through the experience. However, they all enjoy the way the drug makes them feel and the altered state of consciousness they experience. A sense of bliss and peacefulness is a natural consequence of attuning to the Higher Self. This is a state that anyone could find addictive. Eventually a person on the spiritual path never leaves this state of bliss and happiness. However, a drug user must continually use drugs to maintain the altered state that makes them feel good.

Anyone seriously interested in spiritual development should consider joining an organized group that practices yoga, meditation, or some

41

form of spiritual study. The Association for Research and Enlightenment (A.R.E.) is an excellent organization that offers various courses
and study groups that meet at locations throughout the country. Kevin
Ryerson has said that joining an A.R.E. study group greatly helped him
open to channeling. There are many other organizations that might be
local for you to attend. I've listed the addresses for the A.R.E. and
others in the appendix.

What to Do About the Problem—
The Question of Legalization

Now let's get back to the basic issue: What should we as a society
do to combat the threat of drug abuse? Fundamentally, we cannot
attempt to suppress the natural expression of free will. If people want
to take drugs, they will. It doesn't matter what laws are written against
it. That has been proven repeatedly in our history. However, one
argument against legalizing drugs is that legalization sends a message
to the public that the government says it's okay to use drugs. Frankly,
I don't think the public cares about what the government thinks. We
have generally lost respect for most of our government officials. In a
"free" society such as this one, people believe they should be able to
do whatever they want. It is therefore up to the value system of the
individual to dictate what is good and right for them. It is okay for
the government or other organizations to try to influence the values of
the public by pointing out the dangers of drugs, but dictating them as
laws will always be rejected by the masses.

It is up to each individual to decide whether they will make drugs
a part of their experience in this lifetime. Of course, they may be setting
themselves up for a life of misery, but through suffering we learn and
grow from our mistakes.

Since the decision is really up to the individual, drugs should be
legalized to take the criminal element out of their sale and distribution,
and to make it easier for an addict to seek help. When this occurs,
the present media campaign against their use should be stepped up, and
the schools should continue to educate our children about the dangers
of drugs. Most importantly, parents must counsel their children about
drugs, and set a good example at home by not using drugs themselves
and by not abusing alcohol.

Cosmic Awareness has suggested that instead of condemning a
young person for using drugs, they should be encouraged to do
something better, that will be more fun and rewarding. Awareness has

indicated that the proper way to legalize drugs would be to sell them only by prescription through clinics or doctors, and only to people who have an addiction. The price should be required to be very low. This would entice the addict to get the drugs through a regulated outlet rather than the more expensive and dangerous pusher on the street. Thus, legal distribution will eventually destroy the criminal black market that currently exists.

The fact is that whoever wants to use drugs, will use drugs. The government or anyone else can't stop them. However, by warning everyone the best we can about their dangers, maybe we can at least stop the casual drug user, or the one who just wants to be one of the crowd, from making a mistake that could lead to drug dependence and physical and psychological turmoil.

There is some research that suggests that meditation can be effective in reducing drug use among addicts. A 1981 study by Martin R. Wong, Nancy B. Brochin, and Kay L. Gendron reported in the *Journal of Drug Education*, showed that as long as a group of people dependent on drugs or alcohol continued meditating, they were able to reduce their substance abuse. They were also reportedly less paranoic, and more satisfied and self-aware. Perhaps this was possible because the subjects found the natural high one achieves during meditation a more satisfying substitute for the chemically induced kind.

It has also been suggested that many young people who take drugs possess a reckless, carefree, risk taking attitude because they can't envision a positive future. Awareness suggests this belief stems from growing up in the nuclear age, where for the first time in human history, total annihilation of the race is a possibility. Why try to better one's life when some bozo with a button probably will blow us all up soon anyway? As Awareness has stated:

> **This Awareness indicates as it is, there are many who doubt the future will ever come, that they may never see a future. That if one does not foresee a future of reasonable length, then one is not likely to create long- term goals, and if one does not have long-term goals, then the entity is more likely to seek short-term pleasures, momentary pleasures, momentary gratifications, and may be irresponsible towards the world itself, toward society and toward others. (CAC 89-2)**

Awareness suggests that this attitude must be reversed. We must teach the young people that humanity and the Earth can survive, and we will make certain it does survive.

Prayer for Healing the Drug Problem

Dear Father, help us to know thy purpose in all that befalls us. Help us to have the strength to surmount the difficulties and obstacles we sometimes encounter in our life, and help us to see your will being done in all of our experiences. Please help those of us who have lost our power to resist the influences of intoxicating substances and give us the strength to overcome. Help us to love ourselves and to appreciate who we are. We thank you for the guidance we have received and continue to receive in our lives everyday. Amen.

Meditation to Heal the Drug Problem

Imagine that you are standing on a city street corner and you are witnessing the sale and use of drugs. Picture a bright ball of white light descending from the sky and hovering directly above this scene. The light is so bright that the people on the street can't help but notice the light. They look up into the light and the light shines down upon them and fills them. This light reminds them of who they really are and their purpose in this world. This light gives them the strength to overcome their addictions and to handle the challenges in their life. They drop the drugs they were holding in their hands and they begin to leave the scene, transformed by the experience of direct contact with the light of spiritual awareness.

Cosmic Awareness Meditation

To help stop the spread of drugs in our society Cosmic Awareness has suggested that we **"Just visualize some generic drug addict holding drugs and paraphernalia, standing by a toilet in which the entire scene is wrapped in White Light and the entity [the drug addict] can either use the drugs, use them up or can flush them down the toilet, but has no way of exiting from the Light and giving them to any other."** (CAC 89-11)

44

CHAPTER THREE

Crime

Crime is a disease in our society that probably has been around since humanity, and seems to have no permanent cure. The present severity of the drug problem and the high rate of poverty are pushing crime to staggeringly high rates. For example, in 1988 there were 35.9 million reported crimes in the U.S., corresponding to one crime every nine tenths of a second. This chapter will address the causes of crime and some reasons why people become criminals.

Why Crime Exists

To find a solution to any problem in our society we must understand why the problem exists and why people choose to experience it. One purpose for bringing our human souls to Earth is to experience the material aspects of Creation. We come here to recognize the importance and usefulness of the densest form of creative energy: physical matter. Our lesson is to experience its usefulness without becoming so caught up in it that we begin to worship it. However, almost as soon as we enter the physical plane we begin to become entranced by its power to do things for us, and we begin to become possessive of it. Shortly after we are born, we begin to recognize certain possessions as our own. Just think how often you hear children who are playing together fighting over what belongs to them. They say things like "That's mine," inevitably followed by "No, it's mine!" By putting a certain value on material things and calling them "ours," we immediately create anxiety over the possibility of someday losing them. By giving things value, we also create in ourselves the feeling of wanting what we have, and unavoidably, the feeling of wanting what someone else has. This is the

45

cycle that results in the negative feelings of greed, envy, and jealousy.

Many people envy the wealthy, and some even resent them. There is a common belief in our society that not everyone can be rich because there isn't enough wealth to go around for everyone to have whatever they want. Many people feel they have been dealt a bad hand in this life and feel cheated by those who have what they don't. They feel the rich have more than their fair share of what this planet has to offer and they shouldn't be allowed to continue with their greed. These feelings of lack and envy fester in the individuals, and they use it to justify their crimes.

Granted, there are a few rich people in this world who seem to have much more wealth than they could ever use. The fact is that 1½% of the population of this country controls one-third of the wealth. However, this is not a reason to be resentful or envious. The truth is that we all can create whatever we want in our lives. Other people having such a great abundance of material wealth does not prevent us from having whatever we need. God's supply is without limit.

If our chosen experiences for this lifetime require us to be wealthy, then our Higher Self will lead us to wealth. If wealth is not part of our chosen experience, then we will not likely ever be monetarily rich. The most anyone should ever ask for is to receive all they need to fulfill their life's purpose. Many of us have probably had past lifetimes when we were rich in order to learn important lessons concerning the benefits and pitfalls associated with wealth.

Most people who commit crimes do so believing that they won't ever be caught. They believe their chances of obtaining what they want are far greater than going to jail, and for some, they may be right. What they do not realize, however, is that their chances of being caught by their own Higher Self is 100%.

The Law of Karma is perfect; it never misses. For every action, good or bad, there is an equal and opposite reaction. Acts such as theft and murder are outward indications of inner confusion or ignorance of a moral principle that must be learned. The Higher Self, responsible for the forward development of the soul, will not let anyone escape the ramifications of their actions. Anyone who commits a crime will suffer a time of great misfortune and unhappiness until they have learned the lesson they are lacking. This does not always occur in one lifetime. It may not begin in the same lifetime as when the act was committed, but it may stretch over several lifetimes. It all depends on the individual, and how long it takes for them to suffer enough to realize that they have caused their own problems.

46

Who Becomes a Criminal

To some extent, we are all a product of our environment. The messages we receive as children from our parents and others, repeated often enough, become part of our subconscious mind and influence how we feel about ourselves. When a parent or society as a whole repeatedly tells you that you are no good, you eventually begin to believe it. Thus, poor parents with low self esteem, or those who are bitter about their troubles and blame the rest of society, often teach their children to have the same thought patterns. Negative thought patterns are very damaging because our thoughts are things, and what we think about ourselves or our environment will eventually manifest itself in reality. The desperation in our parents and our peers often becomes the desperation in ourselves. This is the type of growing environment that helps create the common criminal.

If we were able to eliminate this negative growing environment for children, we would reduce the crime rate dramatically. To make this happen, everyone as individuals must take responsibility for their own situation, stop blaming others, and replace their hatred and envy with love. People who live in the ghetto must learn to love and respect themselves enough to forgive themselves, and move out of the limiting environment they have made. Although this sounds idealistic, I believe it can be accomplished by acknowledging the truth in two simple principles. The first is to recognize that we all are equally important. We were all made from pieces of the one Creator, and we were all created equal in His eye. All who reside consciously on the physical plane have chosen to leave the spiritual kingdom and experience the material world. Each of us chose our own individual path that leads us through lifetimes of ups and downs. Through our chosen experiences of successes and failures we are motivated to learn and grow to avoid repeating previous mistakes.

Our eventual goal is to become perfected God-beings and return to the Creator in that form. We all share the same purpose for our lives, and the same eventual destiny. This makes us all inherently equal. However, we have chosen our own individual paths, and this makes us unique from one another.

The second principle is the need to accept that the present situation, whether we see it as good or bad, is of our own choosing. Because of what we have done or not done in the past, we are experiencing good or bad fortune in the present. The Higher Self recognizes the lessons we have already learned, and the lessons that still need to be learned. Sometimes these lessons are hard ones. However they become more difficult the longer we choose to avoid them. In trying to understand the criminal mind, we must realize that people who believe their situation to be desperate often do desperate things. People who cannot envision a positive life for themselves, often turn to crime as a means to obtain the money that they believe will remove them from that environment. Even with the possibility of getting caught and going to jail, they believe that crime is their last resort and is worth the risk. Cosmic Awareness states this in the following reading:

> **An individual who is under great distress, who is threatened in terms of survival, whose security is undermined, whose economic livelihood is in distress, will risk more, become more radical in its behavior, take greater chances and lean toward antisocial actions, or create crimes against humanity, more so than one who is economically stable, has too much to lose by being radical, and the more conservative they are in their behavior.** (CAC 90-1)

It is obvious that a strong link exists between poverty and crime. Poverty breeds desperate people. We therefore must reduce the amount of poverty to reduce the amount of criminals. As stated in the chapter on poverty, this can be done by helping people to recognize their own importance and potential, and by giving them every opportunity to make a contribution to themselves and society.

Drug abuse is also an obvious factor in crime. As people become addicted, they become increasingly desperate to maintain their drug supply. Drugs also make it more difficult to find the inner strength to improve oneself. Unfortunately, drugs, poverty, and crime complement one another so very well. Poverty is the cause of the desperation, drugs are the means of temporary escape, and crime is the means of sustaining the illusion of escape.

Although a person's environment can contribute toward one's tendency toward crime, drugs and poverty cannot be blamed for creating all the criminals in society. Certain people with good homes and parents still become criminals almost as a matter of destiny. A person's karma may have a hand in their criminal acts. For instance, a man who murders his own wife, may remember on a subconscious level that she once murdered him. These people are driven by negative subconscious memories from previous lifetimes that were never balanced. They sense subconsciously a need to hurt this other person. The same may apply to robbery, rape, or any crime against another. The only way to break free of these urges and memories, is through forgiveness.

The best way to attain this forgiveness is through prayer. The healing power of intense, meaningful prayer, is such that nothing may overcome it. Pray that you may be forgiven for hurting others and pray that you may forgive those who have hurt you. It also helps while meditating to envision one who has hurt you, and send them healing energy. Imagine their face surrounded by light and send them positive, loving thoughts. Do this so that you may be freed from negative karmic ties with others. Through the power of forgiveness your life ceases to operate under the Law of Karma and begins to operate instead under the Law of Grace. Remember Jesus said, *"For if you forgive men their trespasses, your heavenly Father also will forgive you; but if you do not forgive men their trespasses, neither will your Father forgive your trespasses."* (Matthew 6:14-15)

Jesus gave examples of how we should react to one who hurts us, saying, *"You have heard it said, 'An eye for an eye and a tooth for a tooth.' But I say to you, do not resist one who is evil. But if anyone strikes you on the right cheek, turn to him the other also; and if anyone would sue you and take your coat, let him have your cloak as well; and if anyone forces you to go one mile, go with him two miles."* (Matt. 5:38-41) By giving a person even more than they would try to take from us, we are severing any possibility of a negative karmic link between them and us. Now the person did not steal from us, but instead we gave to them more than they even asked for. Therefore no crime was committed. Such an act of extraordinary love and forgiveness has the power to transform and heal those who would do us harm.

Prison Reform

Most people who commit crimes have some bitterness inside them. They have let themselves become consumed by their own hatred and have no room for forgiveness. Without room for forgiveness, there is no room for God in their life. Having lost touch with God, they become like cancer cells in a body, which do not respond to the will of the brain. The only way to rid a body of cancer is to remove the cancer cells from it. However, unlike cancer cells, people can be transformed into healthy cells and then placed back into the body.

Unfortunately, little actual transformation is occurring within our prisons today. Many "rehabilitated" criminals continue their life of crime when released from jail. Although the system claims to be trying to reform these people, its successes are few. Something is missing in this process. The sad statistic is that sixty percent of all inmates released from state prisons are arrested for committing a serious crime again within three years.

The public shows that it does not have faith in the prison system to reform criminals when it continues to judge ex-convicts on their previous transgressions. For example, most employers will not hire ex-convicts because they do not trust them. Thus, many "reformed" criminals revert back to their way of crime.

The first change that must be made is to stop treating prison as a place where people go to be punished for the length of their sentence, and then released regardless of whether they have been successfully rehabilitated. Instead, people who commit crimes should be removed from society for as long as it takes for their rehabilitation to be successful. All sentences should be identical in length. Punishment should not be the prison's objective. Instead, its objective should be transformation through inner healing. When a prisoner is transformed from destructive to productive, they can then be released.

Second, our current system of justice operates without regard to the Law of Karma. Since our society as a whole is ignorant of this law, it is felt that justice must be carried out by man, rather than leaving it to God. Instead, we should have more faith in God, and operate in harmony with His laws, not outside them. For instance, the death penalty is clearly an abomination in the eyes of God. People remain alive on this planet for as long as there is an opportunity for them to learn something in this lifetime. A natural death occurs when all they have come to do is accomplished, or when they have gotten so far off track that they need to begin again. These decisions are made by the Higher Self, which is far wiser than any judge or jury. Jesus warned us not to judge others when he said, *"Judge not, that you be judged. For with the judgement you pronounce you will be judged, and the measure you give will be the measure you get."* (Matthew 7:1-2)

Let me remind you of a biblical story that illustrates this point. An adultress was brought before Jesus and was about to be stoned by the people when Jesus demanded, *"Let him who is without sin among you be the first to throw a stone at her."* (John 8:7) His point was that we, all who are sinners ourselves, are not qualified to punish other sinners.

By taking a person's life simply to remove them from society, we have not truly gained anything. When we execute a person's body, we have not eliminated that person from existence, we have only sent their soul on a journey into other planes. These are the same planes that we occupy after we die. And since we are all immortal, this person may soon reincarnate on the Earth in another body anyway. Therefore, nothing has been accomplished unless they are able to learn from the experience of being executed. More likely, this will only intensify their hatred. Criminals will remain criminals until they choose otherwise. We cannot change that by killing them.

Although every person is responsible for themselves, we can help those who are losing the struggle between good and evil to win. The main thing that criminals must learn is that everyone is held accountable for their actions. Everyone is judged, not just by society, but by their own Higher Self. Life does not end if one kills themselves or is killed by another. Their deeds remain with their soul. Every negative act is met by misfortune in the future. The situation one is in now is a direct result of the deeds they have performed in the past. There is no one to blame but self. This is the first lesson that a criminal must learn before they can be rehabilitated.

The Association for Research and Enlightenment (A.R.E.), in Virginia Beach, sponsors special study groups in prisons across the country. The program is called the "Over the Wall" prison program and currently distributes spiritual material to over 600 prisons and jails. Study groups are operated within sixty-eight of these currently. A major teaching of all of the Edgar Cayce study groups, whether conducted in prisons or in homes, is that, **"We create our own destiny through the laws of cause and effect."**

Karma is the tool we use to bring us back to our source of perfect divine love. Karma shows us that if we act inharmoniously within society then we will be shown the pain this causes as it is reflected back toward us. This teaching is a missing factor in criminal rehabilitation. This is what must be taught and understood before a transformation can occur. Not just prisoners, but all human beings must learn this lesson as part of their own growth. When this is accomplished, crime will be eliminated, wars will no longer take place, and the world will be filled with only loving, caring, concerned people. Cosmic Awareness defines love for us in the Law of Love:

> *The Law of Love is that law which places the welfare and the concern and the feelings of others above self. The Law of Love is that close affinity with all forces which you associate with as good. The Law of Love is that force which denies the existence of evil in the world, that resists not. Love is the path of least resistance.*

The Law of Love, as given by Awareness, contains within it all the things I have mentioned. How could evil exist if everyone knew in their hearts that if they sided with evil, rather than good, there would come a day of reckoning when this evil would strike them? Obviously, to follow good, or love, is the path of least resistance for anyone. This encompasses within it the answer to that highly complex, virtually unfathomable question: What is the meaning of life? The meaning of life is this simple: **The meaning of life is to discover that following the will of God is truly what is best for us.** That's it! Now it's no longer a mystery.

Finally, the general atmosphere of prison life must be changed. A prison should seem more like a school of higher learning than a holding cell. An environment conducive to creative thinking must be provided. The prisoner should be carefully taught and allowed to study the universal spiritual laws and principles while they are separated from the material temptations of the outside world. They should be helped to understand the Law of Karma and how they have created their own misfortunes. After some time, when they have begun to digest this material, they should be encouraged to apply their new learning in relationships with fellow inmates (students). New prisoners, who are just beginning their studies, should be separated from the others until they have progressed to the point where they will not be a disruptive influence.

Once having studied and then successfully applied the spiritual teachings, the prisoner will begin living by these principles in jail. They will relate to their fellow students with greater understanding, compassion, and forgiveness. When this occurs, their transformation will be complete and they should be ready to reenter society. I believe if these things are done, then our prisons will become more peaceful and more productive. However, all of this is hard to achieve in a place where punishment for crimes committed is still the objective. The objective must be for the inmates to understand the hurt their actions have caused and be truly repentant, never wishing to hurt another again.

Fortunately, groups such as the A.R.E. are beginning to introduce these ideas into prisons. Bo Lozoff, author of *We're All Doing Time*, has begun a prison ashram project where convicts learn meditation and yoga in the Eastern tradition. He gives out free copies of his book and a newsletter to all inmates who request it. He estimates that his materials are in more than 1,000 prisons worldwide. Psychologist Al Nagy has begun to put some of Lozoff's ideas into practice in the Federal Correction Institution at Bastrop, Texas. There are currently 200 inmates involved in the program there, and Mr. Nagy says that some prisoners have gone through dramatic changes, even going as far as forming their own groups to help people in the community. What is most missing in a criminal's life is a sense of spirituality. Programs such as these teach prisoners of their own divinity. When they are opened to feel divine love, then they are healed. The prisons then serve as a place where these things can be learned and felt away from the distractions and temptations of society.

52

Law Enforcement

Now that I have outlined an adequate prison system where true rehabilitation can occur, how do we get the criminals into it? Although our present system of law enforcement has been successful in filling our prisons to well above capacity, many genuine tragedies occur in the process. Very often police stakeouts and arrest attempts lead to shootouts. Police are killed and wounded in the violence nearly as often as the criminals.

When a police officer kills a criminal, they are taking upon themselves negative karma that will eventually need to be balanced. By killing anyone you deny them further experiences in this lifetime that are necessary for their growth. This may come back to you karmically by your own lifetime being cut short by another.

Although society believes that police officers act on the side of good and justice, they are not immune from experiencing the repercussions of their actions. Simply because society judges killing a drug pusher in self defense as acceptable, this does not mean that God does. The sixth commandment simply states *"THOU SHALL NOT KILL."* It does not say, "Thou shall not kill except in self defense, or when a bad guy is getting away, or in times of a drug war, etc." Killing is wrong for everyone, all the time, no exceptions.

We are all sparks of the one divine energy and we all share in the same mission of soul evolution and union with God. Every person, even the criminals, will complete this journey. People who are criminals are very much separated from God, experiencing the opposite extreme of two polarities. But eventually the pain of living this way will be too much for them. Someday they will hit rock bottom and begin looking for the way into the kingdom of heaven.

Capturing criminals without resorting to violence is a challenging task, especially when they have no qualms about killing the police officers. However, to protect the officers from negative karma, there should be greater effort to use nonviolent techniques like nets and stun or tranquilizer guns. Remember, this is protecting the officers as well as the criminals. Police must become aware of their own karma and be careful not to tie themselves to future experiences with these criminals.

The main objective of our law enforcement agencies should not be to terminate the criminals, but to remove them safely from society so that they stop hurting themselves and others. If our prisons are successful in rehabilitating them, then maybe the criminals will eventually reduce in number, and our society will become more peaceful. Unfortunately, people cannot be forcibly rehabilitated. Each person has been given free will by God, and they are not subject to anyone else's. As I stated before, they have to hit rock bottom before they begin to change. The best we can hope to accomplish is to help them recognize that they do not have to fall any further into darkness. They can choose to be transformed at any time and they do not truly need to hit rock bottom. The choice is up to them.

Healing Our Society of the Disease of Crime

Fortunately, there is one action we can all take that will help to make our society more peaceful. This action is the practice of meditation. Besides the peace and tranquility that meditation can bring to the individual meditator, it also can bring these qualities to the consciousness of others. There have been several scientific studies that have shown that meditation by a group of people is effective in reducing the crime rate in the surrounding area. For example, Elaine and Arthur Aaron, in a 1981 issue of *Perspective on Consciousness and Psi Research,* reported on an experiment conducted with a group of meditators in a high-crime neighborhood of Atlanta, Georgia. They meditated for one hour per night for six nights. During that period the crime rate fell dramatically in their surrounding area. The experiment was repeated twice with similar results. On all three occasions, the rate of violent crime dropped between eighteen and thirty percent.

How is it possible that meditation affects crime? A false belief that most of us have is that because we have separate physical bodies we are all separate individuals. Although we cannot physically see connections between ourselves and others, these connections exist in what psychologist Carl Jung called the "collective unconscious." Our conscious mind, where our attention normally resides while awake, appears to make us distinct from one another. However, this separateness does not exist in the higher levels of our mind. Return now to the diagram of the model of the human mind given in the chapter on drugs. This model shows that we are attached to the infinite wisdom of the superconscious mind through our subconscious. On this level we are not separate, because on this level we are all one with the infinite eternal God. By attuning ourselves to this infinite consciousness through meditation, we are bringing awareness of His presence down to the conscious level, where others may also perceive it.

This awareness can be directed toward and felt in the subconscious minds of others. This is the principle through which psychic healing takes place. In order to heal others, or heal the drug problem, or heal the criminals, we must bring awareness of our divine nature and origin to our lower selves. We can awaken this awareness in others by visualizing a white light surrounding them as we meditate. Since in meditation we are in contact with the Higher Self, our connection with the universal mind, we can direct this awareness through our will toward the mind of another.

To have an impact on crime, we can simply visualize a white healing light surrounding our neighborhood, and surrounding all those who inhabit it. We also can envision this light surrounding our prisons, and all the prisoners inside. This technique can be an effective healing tool in all aspects of society. For example, we can envision healing energy being sent to the Middle East to end wars there, or we can send it to all people who are addicted to drugs or alcohol.

We can even make our visualizations more sophisticated if we like. It is important to realize that through meditation and visualization, a small group of individuals has the power to heal whole nations. The crime problem can be healed. The drug problem can be healed. The whole world can be healed. However, transformation can only occur if people want it enough and begin to visualize it. Most importantly, everyone must become consciously aware of their divine nature. Through this awareness, they will know that anything can be accomplished.

Prayer for Illumination

Dear Lord, from whom all blessings come, help us to have whatever we need to accomplish our life's purpose. Help us to love and respect ourselves and recognize our importance as servants of your divine will. Help us to be ever in touch with our oneness with each other and all of creation. We thank you for those experiences in our life that have brought us closer to you. Bring us understanding so that we may refrain from judging others. Help us to be forgiven for hurting others and help us to forgive those who have hurt us. Also help us to give freely to those who would take from us. We thank you for the strength in your wisdom and guidance, Lord. Amen.

Meditation to Heal the Crime Problem

First, close your eyes and visualize a high crime neighborhood. See a huge ball of golden and white light approaching this region from outer space. As it comes closer, the neighborhood becomes brighter and brighter. See the light fill the buildings fill the people in this neighborhood. See the people look to the sky in recognition and total awareness of the divine force. Next, see the white light approach and fill a prison. All of the occupants of this prison are suddenly struck with the realization of their divine power to create their reality. Finally, allow yourself to picture someone who has hurt you at some point in your life. Picture the ball of white light hovering above their head. See the light beginning to descend upon them and surround and fill them. Now imagine that you are talking to this person. Tell them that you forgive them for whatever they have done to you. Ask them to explain to you why they hurt you. Listen for their answer and understand the difficulties this person must be experiencing in their own life. Now see this light filling you and healing any resentment or negative feelings you have toward this person and any other. Stay in this state awhile, and keep this light always inside you.

CHAPTER FOUR

Laws and Government

The entity John has stated through the channel Kevin Ryerson that "Laws are a consensus as to common values." People dictate the laws of society according to the values they hold in common. Thus, the only laws that should exist are the ones that are consented to by the people. Unfortunately, in most governments, the people abdicate their right to create their own laws by turning the responsibility over to government officials. To get elected, these officials often misrepresent themselves during campaigns, and end up doing the opposite of what they originally promised. Often, special interest groups coerce and pressure the elected officials to make laws that benefit and support their interests. The officials agree even when these laws are not in the best interest of the whole nation.

The Laws of Man or The Laws of God?

Throughout this book many concepts are expressed in terms of spiritual or cosmic laws. These laws are the only laws we need to follow to live in peace and harmony. For if we follow the laws of God we could never cause another living creature harm. Jesus summarized all the laws we need to know in two commandments: " . . . *The first is, 'Hear, O Israel: The Lord our God, the Lord is one; and you shall love the Lord your God with all your heart, and with all your soul, and with all your mind, and with all your strength.' The second is this, 'You shall love your neighbor as yourself.' There is no greater commandment than these."* (Mark 12:29-31)

These laws are all we need because they express the awareness that we are all one. The Lord is one, meaning the Lord God is one with us! Love your neighbor as yourself. Why? Because your neighbor is yourself. When this is understood, and becomes the basis of one's values, it is not possible to transgress against society.

Since total acceptance of these laws has not yet occurred, humanity has found it necessary to create its own set of man-made laws and justice. Man-made laws are needed for as long as we continue to be ignorant of the higher laws of God. In principle, the laws of man are a reflection of the morals of the majority. Our government is the group of people chosen to decide what these values are and create laws to uphold them. Although these laws should represent the ideals of the majority, often laws are made that only benefit a few. These few are those who are considered powerful, either politically, monetarily, or both.

Creating a True Democracy

In the U.S. constitution, the founding fathers created a congress of representatives to make the laws of the country. The intention was to have the individual members of the congress represent the ideals and concerns of the different regions of the country. It was necessary to have this type of democratic republic, rather than a true democracy, because the time required for all the people to be informed and vote upon every issue would have been enormous. Nothing would have ever been done quickly without an elected body collected in one place.

In those times, communications across the country were very limited. However, since then we have seen the invention of the telephone, radio, television, satellites, and the computer. We now have bridged that communications gap. With that limitation gone, we can choose to govern ourselves directly, without relying upon representatives. Spirit has prognosticated that in the near future the legislative branch of the government will be obsolete. Computer technology will allow us to have government based upon referendums of the people. In fact, the technology is here today for us to put such a system in place.

Let us picture for a moment, a twenty-four hour nationwide television network. On this channel the issues facing our nation are presented. This channel could be similar to C-Span, which is currently carried on most cable systems. The difference is that those on this new channel don't vote on the issues in place of the people, the people vote for themselves. The issues are discussed on this network just as they are currently discussed in Congress every day without our direct participation. The issues to be voted upon may be selected by a committee or by a referendum of the people in the form of petitions. On the television screen viewpoints both pro and con are discussed by representatives from both sides of the issues. These discussions will be taped and replayed at different times to be certain that everyone will

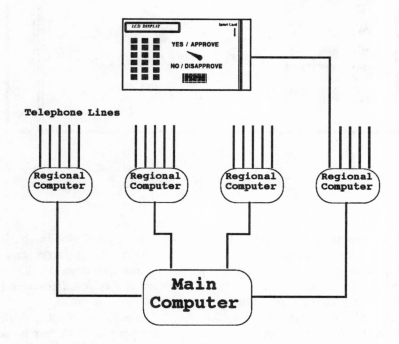

The In-Home Voting Computer Network System

have a chance to watch and decide if they choose. Each week new issues are presented to be voted upon. Of course, the issues will be debated by the news media as well, and this will give them even greater exposure and diversity of opinions.

Now imagine a small box in every household. Each box consists of a switch to select the issue to be voted upon, and a button to select either yes or no. Any time during the week the box may be used to vote on the current issues. These boxes are connected via the telephone lines to a main computer system. Each registered voter is issued a card with a magnetic strip that contains an identification number. To cast

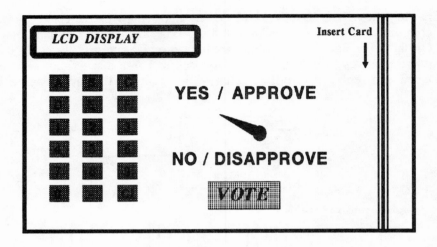

The In-Home Voter Box

a vote, a person must first slide their card through a slot in the box that contains a magnetic card reader. In addition, these boxes can be installed in hotels or other public places so that one does not have to be at home to cast a vote. The same system can be used for electing government officials or voting on issues.

The advantages of such a system are numerous. The most important benefit is the return of the government to the people. With our present society as it is, people are willing to have representatives conduct the government and vote for them because they are too busy with their own issues of daily life. The down side of representatives is that they often do not vote in accord with the majority opinion of their region, but with their own personal opinion. They are also influenced by lobby groups that contribute to their election campaign funds.

With the computerized system I have described, the opportunity for political abuse is eliminated. This new system makes it a quick and simple matter for all people of the nation to participate in the making of their own laws. The same system also could be expanded to incorporate the state and local governments.

With the present system of elections, only a small percentage of the eligible voters turn out to the voting booths. As an example, only fifty-three percent of the registered voters participated in the 1980 presidential election. With a computerized in-home system and the ability to vote directly on the issues that affect them, I believe that the level of participation would definitely increase. People will finally be able to stop blaming the "crooked politicians" for their dissatisfaction, and have only themselves to blame.

The Tax System

With such a voting system in place, I believe the people will vote to make some major changes in our present form of government administration, beginning with the tax system. The worst thing about the present system is that too much effort and human energy is wasted on the collection of taxes. The government has both passed and rescinded many tax laws that encourage people to buy houses, save for retirement, invest in businesses, etc. By putting all these loop holes into the tax system, the process became so complex that the average American needs to hire the services of an accountant to plan their financial portfolios and file their taxes for them. People who file their own taxes find that filling out the forms takes at least one day, and saving all the proper receipts for tax deductions is a year-long process. Also, people who don't use a tax accountant usually end up paying more taxes than those who do, simply because their knowledge of the tax system and all its quirky loop holes are not as complete as an accountant's.

Besides all the tax accountants and advisors who make their living from the system, there are also the employees of the Internal Revenue Service who must review the forms, check all the information, and audit people where necessary. Supporting the incomes of all these people is a burden on the nation's productivity. Their jobs are not connected to the production of any useful goods or services. Thus, their salaries are pure overhead, and must come directly from the taxpayers. There is a huge waste of time and money spent on the collection of taxes, which should be a very simple procedure.

Fortunately, public pressure in the past few years has begun the process of tax simplification. Still, we are far from the ideal. Even with the many accountants and I.R.S. agents who make their living off the tax system, every American is still personally responsible for their taxes and must plan their finances on the basis of their taxes. Taxes are a year 'round concern for most people. For example, whenever an investment opportunity arises, one of the first considerations must be the tax liability or advantage. Most people who wish to invest money have a tax consultant, another person who thrives on the tax system.

Ideally, investments should be made based on where the greatest need lies, not on the largest tax deduction. Another continuous tax concern is the saving of tax deductible receipts and keeping proper records of all possible deductions. All of this energy spent for the sake of taxes is tremendous.

Another problem is that our current system places the major tax burden on the middle class American. No one expects the poor to pay very much in taxes, although they should have to pay their fair share. As I mentioned in the chapter on poverty, each person must be made to feel important by contributing to society as an active participant. Excluding them from paying taxes only feeds their belief of helplessness. The wealthy don't presently pay much in taxes because they are able to invest their money to exploit loopholes in the system. Thus, the middle class is left to shoulder the greatest tax burden.

It is a common practice in business for companies, which make millions of dollars per year in income, to pay little or no taxes. This is because they offset their income by investing the money back into the business, usually for expansion, or buying out another company. Thus, the company ends up with no net income left. The company does not have to pay any tax, and the owners of the company don't have to pay any tax on the business revenues either. The same technique is done by individuals who are able to offset their income by spending it on tax deductible investments.

Without these loopholes, however, the wealthy are penalized for having an abundance of income. They are asked to pay taxes at a higher percentage rate than the average person, simply because they have been more successful in their business life. Penalizing people for being successful is obviously counter productive, since if people are not motivated to start businesses and create jobs, there will be fewer opportunities for everyone else to have what they need.

An ideal tax system is one that is so simple that the individual does not even have to think about it. Without tax concerns, individuals can have more time to be productive in their lives. The ideal system is also fair to all the people. I believe a federal sales tax comes closest to these ideals. With sales taxes there are no forms to fill out, no loop holes to exploit, and no worries for the individual. There is also no way for an individual to cheat on their taxes, since they are not directly involved. The only possibility for cheating arises if the merchants fail to collect the tax. Unfortunately, there is no way to force merchants and their customers to be honest. In any system there will be those who will seek to exploit it. However, it is up to each merchant to decide whether avoiding paying taxes is something they can live with morally.

Since any system will have this weakness, I believe the best system is the one that consumes the least manpower. Certainly the reduction in the work load of I.R.S. agents and tax accountants would alone be enough to justify switching from an income tax to a sales tax. As in any business, the economic success of an organization is directly related to its efficiency. The best way to improve efficiency is to reduce overhead. Tax agents and accountants are clearly overhead that can be reduced with a simplified tax system. This would be less economic burden on the country and government, and thus it would improve our economy.

A sales tax is fair to everyone because it is directly proportional to how much one spends. The rate is the same for everyone, but the wealthy will obviously contribute much more in taxes because they spend more. I believe most people will find this system more acceptable and much less complicated than what we have now. However, I don't see this being manifested until the people of the nation have regained control over the right to make their own laws.

The Fall of Communism

In other sections of this book I have stressed the importance of our gift of free will. It is through our free will that we are able to grow as spiritual beings. It is very important that we do not abdicate our free will to others. A form of government in which others make the decisions that affect our lives, reduces the power of our individual free will and creates resentment within the society. Communist governments that dictate an individual's role in society and attempt to keep everyone on an even economic keel, can never work for long. People choose to be rich or poor to learn their individual lessons in this lifetime. By oppressing the free will of the people of the country, they are taking away their reason for living. Everyone must be free to choose their own path and their own fate, otherwise no spiritual development can occur.

Sweeping political reform is finally occurring in Eastern Europe and the former Soviet Union. People are protesting their oppression, and the governments are beginning to yield. Inevitably, all people everywhere must live free.

One World, Under God?

To ensure that people all over the world maintain their freedom, and don't fall prey to oppressive dictators or governments, a form of world government needs to be established. Awareness has stated that this world government could be modeled after our own form of government in the United States. The United Nations would occupy duties analogous to those of the legislative and administrative branches of our government, and a World Court could be created that would be equivalent to the judicial branch of the U.S. government.

In this structure, the United Nations would decide which are the important issues facing the countries of the world, and would initiate and coordinate multinational efforts to address them. For example, the United Nations should be the focal point for creating and organizing a global effort to heal the environment. Countries would vote on plans to work together as members of a unified globe. If they choose, the people of the member nations could participate in voting on these world resolutions with the In-Home or other voting system.

This new world government also would include the addition of a World Court that would provide the teeth to enforce the agreements that are reached in the United Nations. The inability to enforce its decisions has been what has rendered the United Nations virtually ineffective as a governing body until now. The World Court should be given the power to levy economic sanctions against any national government that does not act in the best interest of its people or the globe. Thus, if a government is found violating the human rights of its people, then the World Court could declare that member nations would restrict trade with that country until their violations have ceased.

All countries of the world should have an open invitation to join the World Government. As an incentive to join, the member nations would enjoy favored trade and economic growth by working in harmony with one another. The independent countries that do not wish to become a part of the union, will not receive these benefits. The economic advantages in becoming a member of the World Government should eventually lead to a unified globe. When this occurs, human rights and the environment must be the central issues that this body of nations must address. In such a world, oppressive dictators could never maintain control, since the political and economic pressures levied on them by the unified nations would be too great.

One difficulty with the beginning of this world government, would be that the most developed and wealthy countries would initially have greater influence and power. However, if this world government is managed by enlightened people, the emphasis would not be to make one's own country greater than another, but to help all countries thrive. Awareness has stated that some division of this government should be devoted to oversee the exchange of money, and the creation of a form of world currency also should take place. The World Government should be able to make certain that the resources of the planet are distributed based on need, rather than the highest bid. In such a system, a country's worth would be in proportion to the products and services it can provide to the collective pool. The more it can provide, the more it should be able to receive from others. Those countries that do not have much should be assisted in their development so that they can become active contributors. Thus, the world economy may not be based on currency backed by gold or another resource, but it could be based solely on the exchange of goods and services.

The idea of a world-wide governing body harmonizes well with the belief in the oneness of humanity. Before the technological advances in communications and transportation of today were achieved, many nations of the world were isolated from one another. Thus, a single world government was unfeasible, and the world was forced to remain in isolated individual pieces. However, now we can choose to give up this fragmented structure and unite for the benefit of all, living in recognition of our oneness with one another and all that exists.

The Oneness of All

The physicists of the twentieth century have been working very hard at discovering the nature of matter. They have built huge particle accelerators to break down the atom into smaller and smaller particles. Their goal is to find the fundamental building block upon which our physical universe is based.

However, in this research, physicists have uncovered some unexpected phenomena that point to the likelihood that some sort of "quantum wholeness," as it was termed by Niels Bohr in the late 1920s, governs the world of the atom. Experiments which led to this theory showed that particles on the quantum level can instantly communicate with one another even when separated by space. As a result, scientists found out that they could not observe a particle or measure its properties without themselves affecting the measurement. This is because the particle is in immediate contact with its environment, and when the experimenter tries to observe the particle he immediately becomes a part of its environment.

Dr. David Bohm, a renowned theoretical physicist currently with the University of London, has begun to take these new theories of physics and expand upon their implications in society. For example, Bohm believes that our illusion of separateness, and our habit of fragmenting our world into individual pieces, is the root of all problems in our society. In fact, physics has shown that there is no such thing as separateness. Our world as it exists is currently out of balance with the way things are in nature. Bohm believes we should stop placing labels on things and separating things and ourselves from one another. We should realize and accept that all people and all things are actually part of us, since we are all intimately connected on the subatomic level.

What is needed most is a social enlightenment that recognizes this oneness and breaks down the barriers that separate us. This is the only way that we can unite and end conflict in our world.

The Great Debate - The Abortion Controversy

Perhaps no single issue in recent history has gained more widespread debate than that of abortion. Virtually every politician, no matter what office they seek, is asked to state their position on this hotly debated subject. The abortion issue raises many metaphysical questions about the creation and destruction of life. Many see abortion as equivalent to murder. They believe that the fetus is just as alive as any human and deserves the right to life. Others see abortion as an action to get rid of something unwanted; something that is not alive until after birth. Who is right?

The issue is quite simply resolved when one is open to accept the belief in the immortality of the human spirit. Each person on this planet is an immortal being. We experience many lifetimes on Earth and also exist on other realms of consciousness between lifetimes. We move betweem these realms by effectively dying on one plane while being born on another.

When we are prepared to leave the spirit realm and return to the physical realm, we seek to create and occupy a body that will be suitable for our purposes on Earth. When two people on Earth have sexual relations, a door opens up from the spirit realm to the physical. A spirit entity wishing to move into the physical plane can enter this door and create a link with the potential parents. The entity's Higher Self selects the genes needed from each parent, and fertilization occurs.

At this point the consciousness of the entity has not yet entered the womb. However, a partnership has been established. The mother, the father, and the entity are now engaged upon creating a new vessel for a human life in the physical plane. During the period of gestation the entity may tend to move in and out of the womb to supervise the development of the fetus. However, the final linking of the spirit to the body is not complete until after birth.

Thus, abortion is not the same as murder. When one murders, they are forcing the consciousness of an entity out of the body they occupy. When one aborts a fetus, they are simply denying the potential for a spirit to occupy a body. However this does not mean that abortion is not a sin. By denying the entity entrance into the earth plane, the potential parents are telling the entity that it is unwanted. The entity feels a sense of neglect in not being wanted by the potential parents. The sin is in not feeling compassion for the entity seeking to be born. When a couple or person aborts a fetus without regard to the feelings of the unborn entity, they are creating karma between themselves and this entity. By having sex, the couple leaves the door open for an entity to enter according to their own free will. Thus, it is their own fault if someone should pass through this door. Callously forcing the entity out, after enticing them to enter, can emotionally scar that entity. The entity feels rejected, unwanted, and abused. Awareness stated this as follows:

> **This Awareness indicates the tragedy in abortion is not so much the depriving of life, because life cannot be deprived between one plane or another: the tragedy is in the attitudes of the entities who do the aborting, whereby they can be so calloused as to assume that the entity is but an object rather than a god, a human being, a form of deity as great and as valuable as they themselves. (CAC 77-5)**

Few people in our society believe in the divinity of us all. Since most people do not believe in reincarnation, they do not believe that the unborn is one who is just like themselves. They do not recognize that the unborn is a human spirit with many experiences and lifetimes, seeking to gain more experiences on the physical plane. Quite probably, the parents and the unborn entity have even known one another in previous lifetimes. People must learn to recognize their oneness with everyone and everything, including those entities who are not presently on the Earth. To feel compassion for another we must be able to place ourselves in their situation. We must be able to feel as they feel. Can you imagine how it must feel to be that entity who seeks to join you and share experiences with you, only to be flatly rejected without any indication of regret or sorrow?

Thus, the tragedy of abortion is largely based upon the attitudes of the parents toward the entity. If the parents indeed regret that they are not able to go ahead with the pregnancy, and do feel sorrowful about having to reject the entity, then they are eliminating some of the entity's pain and some of the karma. Awareness also states this as:

> **This Awareness suggests the sensitivity felt toward the entity as that which alleviates much of the karma. The hostility sent toward that entity with the attitude of "get it out of here" is that which can bring on greater karma.** (CAC 77-5)

Each entity that arrives on the earth plane requires a certain degree of emotional nurturing during their early development. They require the proper care and guidance to obtain healthy attitudes about themselves and fulfill their life's purpose. To have a baby and then neglect it and not properly nurture it, is perhaps more harmful to the entity then rejecting it before birth.

Putting aside one's own life and goals, for the entrance of another into this plane, is a very loving gift. It is a gift that someone gave to you, and you may now return it to another. However, this gift, if given without love and without proper concern, can result in the newly arrived entity being emotionally undernourished. Their self confidence and their ability to love themselves is threatened if they do not experience love from their parents. Their ability to accomplish what they sought in entering this life, will then be encumbered by their lack of self esteem.

Therefore, only those who truly wish to make the necessary commitment to the proper raising and caring of a child should seek to have one. The prevalence of child abuse in our society is clear evidence that many do not recognize the seriousness of the parental commitment. Only through foreknowledge of the necessary sacrifices and commitment, can people decide whether they are willing to accept the adjustments in their life to accommodate a child. Those who engage in sex, without regard for the consequences, are risking that they will one day be faced with a difficult choice. This will be to decide whether they can truly give to the baby the proper love and attention it needs, or that they cannot be worthy parents and should not have the baby at this time. Either choice can be difficult if the couple was not planning to become parents.

Considering the risks associated with sex, how is it that so many people recklessly engage in sexual acts and become pregnant? The answer of course lies in the enormous pleasures of sex. It seems a cruel test that something so joyful should carry such potential difficulties. But the reason for this can be clearly explained.

The momentary gratification one achieves in sex is linked to the opening of the door to the spirit realms. The orgasm itself is the ecstasy of experiencing a conscious spiritual union with one's own spiritual self and their partner's. The joy one feels is largely due to the sensing of one's spiritual link with the divine. It is said that one is closest to experiencing heaven when they are having an orgasm. The purpose and need for the sexual act is to remind one of their spiritual nature. Most people in the physical world are not conscious of their spirituality and have no direct experience of it. In dreams we may experience contact with it, but we are usually consciously unaware. Only in sex are we feeling the genuine ecstasy of our spirituality. Some people are able to experience this ecstasy while in deep meditation, but these are few.

The need for us to have sex, the drive that compels us to do so, is based upon our desire to return to the realms of our divinity. The need to have sex is based upon the fall of humanity from the Garden of Eden. Notice how Adam and Eve were not aware of their nakedness (their sexuality) until after the fall. There would be no drive for sex if man and woman had not separated from their creator. For in Eden, Adam and Eve were in paradise. Our desire to return to paradise and know the joy of the heavens is what fuels our sexual energy.

Of course, in our present physical realm sex is also necessary for procreation. When Adam and Eve fell from the garden, sex was their door into this reality. Thus, it remains the door through which entities may enter the physical world. However, sex can be a two way street. Just as the door is open for entities to leave the spirit realm and enter the physical one, so may we briefly experience the spirit world through sex. However, many people have separated themselves so far from the Creator that sex is purely physical for them. Many people only focus on the physical sensations and do not truly experience the more profound spiritual benefits. One who does not feel the warmth and compassion of joining with another, but only experiences their own physical gratification, is probably far from achieving spiritual awareness. Focussing on only the physical needs is lust, not love. Lust is the desire for physical gratification without regard for the spiritual experience. A baby born out of a relationship of lust is unlikely to find loving and caring parents. Generally, entities who are attracted to entering this plane through such a relationship are themselves of a lower spiritual character.

Certainly a woman who is raped and becomes pregnant has every right to an abortion. For she did not recklessly leave the doorway open, it was forced open. She should not be forced to bear a child that she did not want, when she had no part in inviting the entity into her life.

The answer to the abortion issue is not to legislate morality by making it illegal, but to educate people on the truth of our spiritual nature. When people can recognize their oneness through their spiritual link, they will feel compassion for all. When this compassion is awakened in a person there is no longer the unfeeling and inconsiderate behavior. They feel equally hurt by any unkind act they perpetrate on another. In this knowledge and true feeling for the entity, the pain and karma of an unwanted pregnancy is lessened. The potential parents can then feel what is the proper decision for the highest good of all.

If the parents decide that they cannot have the baby, it is important that they attempt to communicate this to the entity. In their thoughts and prayers they should speak to the entity and explain their situation. They should express their regret and their sorrow. Remember, this entity is just as alive as any of us. Totally ignoring its existence is the worst one can do in this situation. They should send this entity their love and ask for its forgiveness. Perhaps they will someday give the entity another opportunity to enter this plane when they are more capable.

There is no judgement when one follows the Law of Love and puts the concerns and feelings of others above self. We all must remember to do what is the highest good for everyone concerned. If we follow this simple rule, we will surely find the path back to paradise.

Prayer for Oneness

Dear Father of us all and all that is, help us to remember our oneness with you. Help us to be open to receive your love and to channel it to others. Bring understanding to our minds so that we may bring it to others as well. Help us to recognize our common purpose and to be instruments of change and growth for one another. Lord, in the knowledge and sense of our unification with you, give us the strength to break free from those who would oppress us. As we unite in our recognition of you, help us to unite with one another through mutual understanding and sense of purpose. We thank you for providing us with the opportunity to lead and govern ourselves, and we pray that our lessons of separation bring us into harmony with your will. May your work always be done through us, Lord. Amen.

Meditation on Oneness

Imagine a ball of light located in the center of your chest. See this as a ball of bright white light that is growing and gradually filling your body. It fills your upper and lower chest, your lungs, and your abdomen. See it continuing to grow and fill your throat and your shoulders and arms, your hips, and your upper legs. Now see it filling your head, your ears, and also your knees, lower legs, and feet. See it extending beyond your body in all directions. See it reaching above your head and below your feet. This ball of light continues to grow and fill the room. Now see other balls of light in other people around you. See the light also filling them and extending beyond them. Now your ball of light and their's has grown so big that they are beginning to touch. As they touch they begin to overlap and finally merge into one another. See as many balls of light as you can imagine gradually merging into one another and continuing to grow. Continue this visualization and see the whole Earth gradually become engulfed in this one huge ball of light.

Everyone and everything on the earth is now part of this one ball of light. Notice how peaceful this makes you feel. Feel how much you truly love everyone and everything in God's creation. Stay in this feeling of peace and love, and know that as long as you do, you will always be safe.

CHAPTER FIVE

War

Perhaps the biggest and most important realization one makes on the spiritual path is the realization of their oneness with God and all of creation. In knowing that we are all God we know that we are all one cosmic being. We realize that we are individual cells that may think and act independently on a conscious level, but together we share the universal consciousness of one being.

In the beginning, God divided parts of his own spirit and created our spirits. Although we have fallen out of conscious memory of this link to the divine source, a common purpose still binds us together. This purpose is to return to the source of our creation as completed God beings. The fall of man is wonderfully illustrated in the parable of the prodigal son that Jesus taught his disciples. (Luke 15:11-32) In this story, a man has two sons. One son asks his father for his share of his father's estate and leaves home. He squanders his money on riotous living and finds himself destitute. He returns to his father asking to be one of his servants, since he is not worthy to be called his son. However, his father welcomes him with open arms and gives a celebration in his honor. We are all essentially God's prodigal sons who have taken our individual shares of our Father's kingdom and left Him. As was the father's house in the parable, so is the kingdom of heaven open to our return. Our goal is to return to His kingdom having grown from our experiences separated from Him.

God created all of us as unique individuals to share specific responsibilities as His co-creators. God's plan requires that we all perform our unique individual tasks as part of a team that needs each of its members to accomplish its goals. This team is like that of a living body made up of individual cells, each with specific tasks to perform for the good of the body. The tragedy of war is equivalent to a disease like cancer, where the cells of the body consume one another senselessly. The body as a whole deteriorates when the functions of the destroyed cells are no longer performed. The armies of the world are like tumors that overpower and consume healthy cells and occupy their place in the body. Tragically, human beings have not recognized their oneness with one another and continue to act without regard to others. Likewise, many countries can only see what is best for them, and show little regard for the welfare of others. Consequently, more than 128 million people have been killed in wars in this century alone.

Why War Exists

What reasons could government leaders possibly give to justify starting or entering a war? A common excuse is a boundary dispute over the control of a piece of land and its economic resources. What is so valuable about land that some feel we must kill others (other parts of our self) to have it? Does anyone but God really own the land of the planet? You know the saying, "You can't take it with you." All material things are useless to us after we leave our physical bodies in death. The only important possessions we have are spiritual, since we carry them with us into all our planes of existence. Our karma stays with us from lifetime to lifetime. How then, can anyone ever justify killing other parts of ourselves over material concerns? Is it worth gaining negative karma because of material possessions that are only meaningful during one brief physical lifetime?

While we are on this planet we should share all of the planet's resources equally. I suppose most of us feel we don't share because of greed. Webster defines greed as, "An overwhelming desire to acquire or have, as wealth or power, in excess of what one requires or deserves." So resources such as oil aren't shared because it gives those who possess it wealth and power. But is it the oil that gives the power or is it we who want it? What if we just said to the Middle East, "Fine if you're not willing to charge a fair price for the oil you possess, then we don't want it?" In truth we don't really need their oil. After all, how did we live without it for all those centuries that came before this one? The oil crisis of the seventies was actually a blessing in that it forced us to look harder into alternative energy sources and conservation. It showed us that we did not need as much oil as we were previously using.

Most conflicts occur when one group of people wants to own what another has. This may be their property or their freedom. The Laws of Abundance state that there are enough resources available for everyone to have an abundance. The Higher Self brings to each person whatever they truly need. But most people don't recognize those principles and feel they must struggle to obtain what they want. Many can even justify forcibly taking from another what they want. Instead of trusting the Laws of Abundance, they believe in a law of scarcity, which states that there are not enough resources available for everyone to have an abundance. In order to receive, they believe that you must take from others. A belief in scarcity is what lays the foundation for many wars.

Many wars are also based on religious differences. Often the land that is fought over is considered by one or both sides to be holy land. These "holy" wars are a contradiction of terms. The word holy is derived from the same root as the word wholeness. We are holy when we recognize the wholeness, or oneness, of everything. Religions may have many superficial differences. However, under the surface, we all worship the same deity, which is the source for all life.

The most important possession a person owns is their free will given to them by the Creator. Our free will is what enables us to express ourselves in whatever manner we choose for our highest spiritual growth. When one lives in an oppressive society, their free will is suppressed and their soul development is retarded. Obtaining freedom through war, however, is not the answer. Yes, the United States was founded only after independence from England had been won through the Revolutionary War. But Mahatma Gandhi showed India and the rest of the world that the same results could be obtained through nonviolent demonstrations and disobedience. In a war, much negative karma is created by the soldiers on both sides, but Gandhi's method minimizes this karma.

Nonviolent resistance is the answer to facing dictators. Love is a much greater and more powerful force than violence. It does not matter what a ruthless dictator or other aggressor would take from you. Just do not relinquish your personal will and follow the will of another out of fear. If instead of fighting back violently, we simply refuse to obey someone else's mandates, then we would render them powerless over us. Even if they take our physical life, we would remain free. But we would only be free if we showed compassion and sympathy for such a foolish person and not hate. For if we cannot forgive another we will become like them and get trapped in their web of hatred and separateness.

The purpose of evil is to draw us away from perfecting ourselves in God's image. If a person filled with evil, such as an Adolf Hitler or Saddam Hussein, succeeds in drawing us into violent conflict, then

75

they have already won the battle. They have successfully detoured us away from our struggle to reach perfect love and harmony, by enticing us to respond to their hatred with violence.

The Weapon of Terrorism

A powerful weapon our society is currently combating is that of terrorism. As I mentioned in the chapter on crime, people who believe their situation to be desperate are more likely to do desperate things. The Palestinians, for example, are a people of "have-nots," who don't even have a country. These people are desperate enough to use the weapon of terrorism to make known their cause. Terrorism is currently an effective weapon that requires very few resources, and therefore can be used even by those who have nothing.

Terrorism is only an effective weapon because it feeds on our fear of death. If we eliminate this fear we eliminate terrorism as a weapon. This can only be done by realizing that this life is only a very small part of our total existence. We have lived thousands of lifetimes before, and will continue to live in many different places and times for as long as we choose. No one can take that away from us. Thus, there is nothing to fear about death. According to the testimony of people who have had near death experiences, even the process of dying is nothing to fear. It is common that many people don't even realize right away when they are dead. Therefore, there is nothing to fear in death, and nothing to fear in terrorists. Ignore their threats and this weapon will cease to be effective. However, the real answer for peace in the Middle East is to end the desperation of the people who would attempt this aggression. Perhaps when we overcome our fear of these people, we can begin to help them improve their lives and satisfy their needs.

Meditation is very helpful in controlling our fear. Fear is reduced dramatically in people who meditate regularly. This is because when a person meditates they are balancing the spiritual centers of their body. Fear is based in the lowest spiritual center which controls the operation of the adrenal glands. Fear is rooted in our animalistic survival instinct. Mother nature provides animals with this instinct as a means of self preservation. Humans however, possess the gift of free will, and through the ability to make choices for ourselves we are able to supersede animal instincts. The more one is driven by instinctive reaction, the less control of their life they maintain.

Human beings possess seven spiritual centers in all. The lower three govern over our animal selves. The four higher centers allow us to feel love, express ourselves, consider our spirituality, and finally integrate with God. Through meditation we can awaken our awareness to all of our spiritual centers. Integrating all of our centers together in meditation allows the higher centers to balance and control the lower centers. Through this balancing our instinctive reactions are made to submit to the will of our higher centers. Thus, through this process we are able to control and eliminate our fears.

As we develop spiritually and begin controlling our fear, terrorism will become an obsolete weapon, without any power over us. Cosmic Awareness has indicated that, **"It does appear within a few years that the effects of terrorism will no longer be able to bring benefits to those perpetrating terrorism, and that this will then begin to fade away as a viable weapon for these nations . . . .."** (CAC 90-1)

Wartime Karma

Just think of the karma incurred by the thousands of soldiers in a war. Again, the commandment "THOU SHALL NOT KILL" applies even during wartime. So called "holy wars" are a contradiction in terms. All wars are a sin. Killing is always a sin. Jesus was the pattern for us to follow. Remember that he would not fight the Romans and lead the Jews to physical world freedom. This is what they believed the messiah would do, and they were very angry when he would not. As Jesus said, *". . . all they that take the sword shall perish with the sword."* (Matt. 26:52) Also, it is written, *"He that leadeth into captivity shall go into captivity: he that killeth with the sword must be killed with the sword."* (Rev. 13:10)

Evidence of wartime karma was given in Shirley Maclaine's *Dancing in the Light*, when during an acupuncture session she experienced vivid memories of past lives. In many visions she was a soldier in different times and places. These scenes alternated first with her killing an enemy soldier, and then in the next scene with that soldier killing her. Repeatedly the same action occurred in different times and places. Ironically, during her visions she recognized that soldier as her mother today. These visions showed her the tragedy she lived over and over again in the name of war. This negative karma continued to bind her to her mother until finally they were able to break the bond between them with forgiveness.

Dissolving karmic ties is most easily done when we realize that we are truly immortal beings, destined to live through eternity with our fate governed by our actions. When we begin to see life as a continuous process, we realize that it is much better to be killed than to kill.

How to Prevent Wars by Realizing Our Oneness

Cosmic Awareness has defined the Law of Correspondence as, *"As it is above so it is below, and as it is within so it is without."* This law states that equivalent events and conditions occur in all planes of our existence: within our bodies, our communities, our countries, our planet, and even the heavens.

Each of us is familiar with our own unique physical bodies, separate from one another. Our bodies are made of individual parts known as cells, and these cells are made of even smaller parts. As individuals, we make up the cells of a larger body known as humanity. We are the cells of the living being known as humanity. Humanity is also a cell in a larger body made up of all the living beings in the universe. The Earth is the foundation for our body in the physical plane, and it also is only a single cell among all of the other planets and heavenly bodies which make up the physical universe.

According to the Law of Correspondence, any event or experience that occurs to one of these bodies also occurs to them all. For example, cancer is a disease in which certain cells in the physical body group together and attack and kill other cells. This is analogous to the way armies attack other armies of the world. The individual soldiers are cells in the body of their army, and the armies are cells in the body of humanity. For a body to maintain proper health, malignant cells must be controlled and eliminated from the body, or else transformed into healthy cells. For our world to be at peace, the armies and people that would attack others also must be eliminated. Since people are immortal, the only way this can be done is through transformation. Transformation occurs when one fully realizes their oneness with others and all of creation, as it is demonstrated by the Law of Correspondence. With this recognition they can no longer justify hurting another person for any reason.

Declaring war is the ultimate statement of our ignorance of our oneness. By killing one another we are affirming our belief in our separateness. All of humanity shares the same source and purpose. If we realize that we are all just different pieces of one being, how could we kill other parts of our own self? When one person is harmed, so are we all. That is the realization we must come to before we will have eternal peace.

Often we get patriotic feelings when our country is involved in a war, and society generally considers this positive and desirable. However, we must stop using patriotism as a justification for sinning against God by killing one another. I believe patriotism, as it currently exists, is the worship of separateness, predicated on the feeling that one's own country is better than another. This feeling does not have to continue any longer. It is okay to feel proud about belonging to a particular group of people, but to feel superior is a mistake. To achieve world peace we need to redirect patriotic feelings for our country toward uniting and unifying the planet. Unification occurs when the barriers that separate us and restrict our travel from one place to another are torn down. The United States of America is a unification of fifty separate states. These states are unified because any American citizen can live and work in any state they choose. There are no significant restrictions that regulate travel or business between them. Thus, they function in peace and harmony with one another as one. To unify the world, the restrictions and regulations that keep people from living and working in any country they choose must be eliminated.

Perhaps a good first step to get people thinking about unification across the globe, would be to create a world flag and a world anthem that is taught in the schools and sung at sporting events. These would be expressions of our love and devotion toward our world and one another. The following are lyrics to a song that I wrote one day while contemplating this idea:

This is Our World—
The World Anthem of the Planet Earth

This is our world.
We live in peace and harmony.
This is our world.
Through all lands our brothers we keep.

Break through the falling walls, we can,
Bringing peace through all the land.
Let us carry forth our promises to,
Thee by Whom we live and breath.

This is our world.
No land better than the rest.
This is our world.

IT'S TIME TO MAKE IT HAPPEN ON EARTH

Together under a single crest.

A land so fine as this,
With wings we spread,
To meet thy maker
In His great plan.

As I mentioned in the chapter on government, it is important that a World Government, which includes a World Court, become established. Just as each state in the U.S. maintains its own government, the countries of the world should continue to maintain their own governments. However, representation in a multinational government would be granted to all who would join. The World Court would resolve disputes between nations by settling them in a multinational judicial proceeding. As I previously explained, the Court's decisions would be backed by economic trade restrictions against any nation that does not comply. Cosmic Awareness has indicated that if a World Court was in place at the time, it could have resolved the Falkland Islands dispute, the Iran/Iraq border dispute, and the U.S./Iraq Gulf War.

Armageddon

What will finally bring a lasting peace to this world? For peace to occur there must be a worldwide consensus for conflicts to be settled with reason and compassion. If only one group of people was to adopt these ideals, they would be leaving themselves vulnerable to others who do not accept these beliefs. Thus, the entire world must be ready to embrace peace and practice giving unconditional love to their enemies as well as their friends. For this to occur there must be a raising of consciousness among all peoples of the world.

However most people are not prepared to accept the spiritually-based concepts I have been outlining in this book. They are too involved in their materialistic lives looking for fulfillment when they make their first million. Others are too consumed with just surviving to care about such things. Thus, when conflict occurs, most people react with their animal instincts rather than with the more evolved approaches. Unfortunately, it appears that for so many people to be enlightened, probably everything we value will need to fall apart. When everything we think is important is destroyed, we will finally realize that none of it was worth fighting over.

The following is an excerpt from a teaching by the Eternals given in Henry Leo Bolduc's *The Journey Within*:

(If we, as individuals or as a group, were to decide that there is to be [peace on earth], is that possible?)

Yes, but—and we must stress this strongly—you speak in terms of "is it possible" in your realm of reality. It is possible in our realm or your realm of reality, or anybody's, so to speak. But you must have a group consensus to bring a "peace" that is to everyone, that is to all. A collective peace must be brought about by collective realities converging together for this. That is not to be reached in the near future. There must first be an unbalancing and a total upheaval. Once everything is scrambled, then it can be placed back together . . . .. Things must fall apart. They must be completely destroyed before they can come together.

(How can we best prepare for this scrambling?)

The best way to prepare for it would be to be dead. It's going to be very unpleasant for those that are alive . . . in the physical form. There will be melting of flesh. There will be horrible times. There will be great droughts caused by the radiation and by the screens or the ionosphere being destroyed. There shall be great heat from the sun scorching because of the atmosphere being in such a disarray . . . .. And yet at the very end of this, is when —your society—shall become utopian. Only by being completely destroyed can it be brought back together again.

The teaching went on to say that although the exact time of these events was to be kept secret, it would happen in our present lifetime for many of us. The Eternals also said that some people will live and there will be an immediate altering of their consciousness:

[It is as if some people say] "Oh, my God, the world's blowing up. There must be something else. Wow! Look at all these horrible things happening. I must search for the truth quickly." With enough people thinking this way instantly, the consciousness shall be altered. With enough people wanting the truth, seeking the truth, it can be altered. The whole thing could be avoided if people would simply change their ways . . . .. It can be, but it won't be.

Although the Eternals appear to take a pessimistic view of humanity, they do admit to the possibility of Armageddon being avoided. Spirit has said through Kevin Ryerson that this generation has received the "sign of Jonah." Remember in the Book of Jonah how God commanded Jonah to proclaim to the people of Nineveh that because of their wickedness they were about to be destroyed. However the people of Nineveh repented and God did not destroy them. Thus the "sign of Jonah" is an indication that we must hear this warning of the Eternals if these tragedies are to be avoided.

Let's return now to the Law of Correspondence and the principle that what occurs within also occurs without. Cosmic Awareness has indicated that the war of Armageddon has already been fought and won in the kingdom of heaven:

> **This Awareness indicates there is a great need for entities on this plane to begin spreading the word, that the war of Armageddon, the battle of the internal being is coming to an end. This Awareness indicates that the war between the forces of light and the forces of darkness is ending on the inner plane. The concept of evil is that which no longer exists on this inner plane. And on the outer plane, there is only the memory, the shadow, and the echo, and the fear of evil that remains, and these too are fading. This Awareness indicates that as these fade and entities understand and realize that though error still exists, error still occurs and entities still make mistakes, there is no longer evil, when this is realized this entire plane begins to change its face. This Awareness suggests you also understand that only the reactions and the echoes of those polarities remain on that physical plane. That the word must be spread, that the war is over, that peace has come, that entities may lay down their arms, lay down their swords, lay down their hostilities, lay down their words and battle gear, the battle gear of the various beliefs and religions which create separateness between these forces. This Awareness indicates that you are all One, that you are all souls and cells of this Awareness. That the body of this Awareness is moving into that which is balance and harmony, and that the cells or souls of this Awareness need not struggle against each other.**

Awareness indicates that the path of everlasting peace has now been cleared for us on the inner plane. This inner place is the place of our spirit, the plane of our Higher Self. A part of us always exists on this plane. Our conscious mind does not fully recognize this plane, and thus does not know that the way for peace is clear for us on the inner plane. We can choose to manifest this peace on the outer plane, or we can let the forces of the past continue to flourish. Armageddon does not need to occur on this outer world. The choice is ours.

UFOs and Aliens: An Unexpected Threat

There is, however, a third party involved in the affairs of humans that makes the possibility of Armageddon less clear. This third party I am referring to is the nine different type of alien creatures who are currently visiting this planet, of which five are influential in the affairs of humanity. I realize that stories about aliens are hard for some readers to swallow at this time, and even I have trouble accepting it myself. However, there is much evidence that I can no longer deny. For example, some personal friends of mine have told me that they have clearly seen UFOs, and I have no reason to doubt them. In addition, there are the accounts given by Shirley Maclaine in her book *Out On A Limb*, and the Gulf Breeze sightings of alien ships that are clearly captured on film and videotape. These are only a few examples I can give.

The most important reason for why I have begun to accept the possibility of an alien presence, is that in recent years most Cosmic Awareness messages have been concerning this subject. This is a source in which I have much faith. The whole subject of the alien threat is a very involved one, so I won't attempt to summarize all the information that is available. There are many books and tapes now available besides the many Cosmic Awareness readings that have discussed aliens since 1979. Instead, I will focus on the subject of Armageddon, and how the aliens are adding a new dimension to the picture.

It is important to understand that aliens have been with us since the beginning of human existence on Earth. There are many historical accounts from ancient civilizations of visitors from other planets. In those civilizations the aliens were called gods. Awareness has indicated that we are all ancestors of a race of humans who live in another star system known as the Pleiades. The Pleiadians actually helped to seed the human race on the Earth.

IT'S TIME TO MAKE IT HAPPEN ON EARTH

The Pleiadians are highly spiritually-developed people who have been carefully watching over us since our beginning on this planet. They have been guiding our development, much as a parent guides the development of its children. The Pleiadians still communicate with us and are currently channeled by Barbara Marciniak, who has devoted her life to bringing their message to all who will hear. The Pleiadians also fly around the Earth in space ships and have been seen on many occasions. Clear photographs of their ships were taken in the 1970s by a Swiss man named Eduard Meier. These beings are what could be termed the "good" or "friendly" aliens, and they resemble humans very closely in appearance.

There are, however, four other types of alien beings who are visiting and influencing the Earth, and Awareness warns that none of these are to be trusted. These alien types are based genetically on insects and reptiles, and include those that are grey in color with large almond shape eyes. They come from the star systems of Zeta Reticulan, Orion, Draco, and Belletrax. Unfortunately, many of these aliens are definitely of the "unfriendly" variety, and have as an agenda the enslavement of humanity.

The first modern day contacts with these "unfriendly" aliens, known simply as the "Greys," occurred in the 1940s and 1950s when several alien crafts crashed in the desert. From these crashes one alien survivor was recovered, and was secretly held by the U.S. government. The government decided it was best not to tell the public about these alien contacts, believing it would create mass panic and create severe economic problems. However in 1953, a fleet of alien spacecraft from the Orion constellation began approaching Earth.

About this time, the Pleiadians contacted our government, and warned our officials about the approaching aliens. The Pleiadians offered their help, which focused primarily on increasing our spiritual development. However, they insisted on conditions that our government would not accept. The most critical one was the total destruction of all nuclear weapons. The government, having rejected the help of the Pleiadians, met with the aliens from Orion when they arrived, and established a diplomatic relationship with them. Sixteen people were exchanged for sixteen aliens as ambassadors.

Now let me illustrate how this pertains to the subject of Armageddon. In 1917, apparitions of Mary, the mother of Jesus, appeared to children near the town of Fatima, Portugal, to deliver an important message to humankind. Unfortunately, much of what she said was kept secret by the Catholic Church. However, according to William Cooper, a person who has recently uncovered and released much secret government information, the U.S. government found out about the contents of the messages. The government officials were very concerned about the particular prophecy that Mary gave that predicted the appearance of an antichrist beginning in 1992, and a nuclear holocaust between the years 1999 and 2003. Mary said this would occur unless we turned away from evil and placed ourselves at the feet of the Christ.

Our government, not having this level of faith in humanity to reform, decided to exploit the superior technology of the aliens to form human colonies on other planets, particularly the Moon and Mars, so that at least some humans could escape the holocaust. They also began secret construction of underground cities, which currently do exist, and could be occupied to keep an elite few safe from the nuclear weapons.

Having allied ourselves with the "unfriendly" aliens, the Pleiadians have now begun to pull away from the Earth, leaving us to learn our lessons the hard way. Although the Greys often pretend to be our friends, Awareness warns us that they are likely to become our worst enemy. Believing themselves to be superior to humans, the Greys, and the Reptilians who are to follow, treat Earth as a kind of zoo, or farm, and will soon be attempting to reap their harvest by taking control of the planet and enslaving all of humanity.

Although this alien talk may seem far out to you, at least keep in the back of your mind the warning that Awareness gives to keep away from UFOs, and not to trust any aliens that you may meet. Always remember that we are masters of our own destiny. If indeed these "unfriendly" aliens are seeking to occupy the Earth, it is only because we have attracted them by our own ego-based existence. Everything that happens to us, either as individuals or as a unified body, occurs because it is in our best interest to have those experiences. Perhaps an alien invasion is soon to occur. If it does, it could have the positive effect of forcing all the races and nations of the planet to unite in one strong display of human oneness. However, we must not unite for the purpose of killing the aliens or having a war with them, but for the purpose of greeting them with a unified plan of nonviolent resistance.

Perhaps the higher purpose of an alien invasion would be to teach us a karmic lesson about our own invasions of one another. There have been several analogous conquests and invasions of humans by other humans in our history. A recent example is the conquering of the American Indians by the settlers in the 1800s. The Indians were invaded by an overwhelming number of technologically superior "white" men. The settlers had little regard for the Indians, considering them pagan barbarians. The "white" man felt greatly superior to the Indian. The settlers had many inventions and weapons that the Indians had never before seen. Many Indians fought the settlers and resisted violently, but they were no match for the greater power of the "white" man.

Today there are but a few American Indians left. What was their mistake? It was that they reacted to the settlers with violence, rather than with love. Most Indian tribes professed to be very spiritual people. However, they reacted to the evilness of the settlers with their own evilness and ruthless bloodshed. They did not see in time that they were no match for the settlers and to fight them would be useless.

Thus, we should learn a lesson from what happened to the Indians. If we attempt to combat the aliens with our weapons of today we will be swiftly defeated. It would be as if we were throwing spears and shooting arrows while our enemy was using rifles and cannons. I believe the aliens represent a test for us. Will we fight them with violence and bloodshed as we have fought against our own human aggressors? Or will we grow enough spiritually to recognize that all living beings are one, and that we can combat hate with love? Instead of fighting the aliens we could greet them and try to make peace with them. Of course, they will still probably want to enslave us. But this is when we should begin our plan of nonviolent resistance based upon the principles of Gandhi. Remember how the British could not maintain control over the people of India when they refused to subjugate their will.

No one can truly enslave another unless they give their permission. We are all much more than our physical bodies. Our true selves, our spirit and our soul, are immortal and infinite. They cannot be imprisoned by anyone but ourselves. Jesus really did come to free the Jews from the Romans. However, most people of that time could not see that he was teaching them to free their spirits. They thought that he would lead them in combat and conquer the Romans. But instead Jesus taught that the way to freedom is through the heart, and only those who could see that truth were set free.

There is also another lesson that we may learn from the aliens. Perhaps when the massive government cover-up of the whole alien situation is finally admitted, the public will see the error in allowing the leaders of government and religion to make their decisions for them. Maybe we will learn to stop avoiding responsibilities by pushing them onto others to whom we give our power.

Certainly if the talk of aliens and their pending invasions are true, or if the prophecies concerning Armageddon come true, there are tough times ahead. However, it is through these negative experiences that we choose to learn and grow. I pray that soon we stop resorting to wars and violence to settle our disputes. For when we finally do, we will have learned perhaps the most important lesson of all: Love is the greatest power on Earth, and in the heavens.

Prayer for World Peace

Dear Lord, maker of heaven and earth, grant us peace. Through our recognition and acceptance of our roles as divine beings, help us to seek and find the pathway to harmony and love. Help us to be at one with your purpose and to obtain whatever we need through this attunement. Help us to overcome our fears, Lord, and to know that all our experiences are sent by you for our benefit. Help us to join to together as the one cosmic being we truly are and continue on our journey back to your kingdom. Bless those of us who are aware of your presence and give us the strength and the words to awaken others. May we find peace within ourselves and with others through your divine love. Thank you for the opportunity to serve your holy purpose. Amen.

Meditation for Inner Peace and Overcoming Fear

In this meditation you will visualize the ball of white light moving through and energizing the seven spiritual centers of your body. Begin by imagining that ball of white light somewhere in outer space. With your thoughts draw it toward you and have it hover over the top of your head. Now slowly bring the ball of light down upon your head so it is just touching the top. As it touches you feel this first spiritual center energized and pulsating with light. You may imagine that rays of violet are shooting out of the top of your head. Next bring the ball of light a little further into your head and have it stop when it is even with your eyes and forehead. Feel the region between your eyebrows become energized and imagine rays of indigo light bursting forth. Next bring the ball of light into your throat, and feel it become energized. Sense blue light shooting out of your throat. Bring the light down into your chest now and see green light rays as your heart becomes energized. Continue to lower the light sphere into your solar plexus and feel the energy and yellow light filling and emanating from your solar plexus. Slowly allow the ball of light to reach your navel area and feel this region energized and emanating orange light. Finally, the light reaches the area near the base of your spine, and you feel your spine energized and emanating red rays of light.

Now the ball of light begins moving back upward, and as it reaches each of the seven centers it continues to energize them. Imagine the ball of light moving more rapidly up and down through your body and see it becoming a streak of brilliant white light that is dancing and swirling within your body. All of the colors of the seven centers are mixing together with it. Your entire body is energized and alive.

Continue to feel this energy as long as you like and know that your inner self is being brought into balance and harmony with your higher self. As you feel ready, slowly allow the light to become quiet and peaceful as your body rests and relaxes.

CHAPTER SIX

Health and Disease

In defining health, we should recognize that we must be concerned with more than just our physical bodies. We exist on more than just the physical level. Some refer to the other aspects of themselves as residing on other planes, although all these planes are actually within us. Our physical health is something that is obviously important to all of us. However, many of us tend to overlook the true significance of our bodies as the vehicles of our soul. The body is the physical church that houses God within all of us, and it deserves to be treated and maintained with an amount of respect. This is written in the bible as, *"The body is the temple of the Holy Spirit."* (I Corinthians 6:19) Through the interaction with matter that is possible only when we are in physical form, we are able to grow from experiences that are unavailable on other planes.

A healthy person is one who is balanced on the four planes of self. The planes we are mostly concerned with are the spiritual, the mental, the emotional, and the physical. To function properly on any plane, it is necessary to meet the needs of all the planes. A person who focuses all their attention on any one plane, will suffer from lack on the other planes. This can in turn have a negative impact on even the plane on which they are concentrating their energy. This is what is termed an imbalanced condition.

For example, one who wants to become a saint, and focuses on only the spiritual, will likely suffer from emotional, mental, and physical difficulties. These could manifest as feelings of loneliness and isolation, loss of some mental faculties, and even physical illness. This could then impede their ability to achieve the desired spiritual goal. Conversely, if one focuses all of their energy on building and maintaining their physical body, while neglecting their emotional, mental, and spiritual selves, they are likely to suffer on all levels, and ironically probably will develop some physical illness as a result. Balance on all planes is necessary for a healthy and happy life.

Why Illness Exists

When we become sick it is an indication that we are somehow out of balance within ourselves. Often, physical illness is the only way in which we become conscious of the unbalanced condition. As Edgar Cayce described it, " . . . **all illness is sin . . . ..**" (3395-2) Sin, as it is traditionally defined, is an offense against religious or moral law. However, in the broader sense in which Cayce used it, sin is the following of one's own ego instead of the will of God. Committing a sin always has some sort of repercussion. It may manifest immediately as illness, or may remain as karma that will eventually have to be balanced. The ego is the part of us that believes itself to be separate from God. Following the ego eventually leads to unhappiness and dissatisfaction, for the ego is a lie and its promises always false. If we instead follow the guidance of our Higher Self, which is one with God's will, we will know true happiness and be truly without sin.

The Higher Self can bring to us whatever we need to be happy if we first remove the ego from its path by placing aside our greed and personal ambitions. As Edgar Cayce said, **"For God has not purposed or willed that any soul should perish, but purgeth everyone by illness, by prosperity, by hardships, by those things needed, in order to meet self—but in Him, by faith and works, are ye made every whit whole."** (3395-2)

We truly make our own reality. If we become ill, it is a result of a choice we made that was not in accord with our spiritual ideal. Physical illness is just one of the ways that our Higher Self attempts to balance our misdeeds according to the law of cause and effect. It is not a punishment, but a natural consequence of being out of balance. We are spiritually out of balance when we go against direction of our Higher Self, which is the will of God. We can become mentally out of balance when we harbor negative thoughts about ourselves or others. We can become emotionally out of balance when we fail to express our emotions. We can become physically out of balance when we fail to provide our body with the proper nutrients or exercise. When we become sick it is a signal to our conscious mind that we are in some way guilty of ignoring our Higher Self, which knows what is best for us on all levels. In this way illness can be a reminder and a teacher.

Negative emotions and thoughts are very likely to cause illness, especially when they are repressed. Many of us keep anger we feel toward others inside, especially anger toward our parents or our family. Catching a cold is usually an indication of repressed emotions. According to Cosmic Awareness, " . . . **a cold or flu is an emotion which has been held in check, or a collection of emotions which have been held in check for so long that they are forcing their way out of your system.**" (CAC 87-15) Awareness also points out that the symptoms of a cold, the red eyes, the runny nose, are similar to the act of physically crying. Thus, to heal the psychological factors causing a cold, one needs to experience an emotional release. For this, Awareness recommends as a remedy mint type odors, such as mint tea, to aid in the release of the emotions and the congestion.

Since we need to be able to release our emotions before they become illnesses, psychotherapy can be beneficial for everyone. By treating the blocks and imbalances in our mind, we remain more healthy physically. When we become ill we must recognize that this is an indication of an imbalance of the psyche that must be brought to light.

To stay healthy it is important to remain conscious of one's thoughts, because our thoughts directly create our reality. Negative thoughts can have a toxic effect on the body. As Edgar Cayce said in one reading, **"The thoughts of the body act upon the emotions as well as the assimilating forces. Poisons are accumulated or produced by anger or by resentment or animosity."** (23-3) Once becoming aware of our negative thoughts, we can transform them before they impact the emotions and solicit a negative physical response. This is done by viewing a displeasing situation or person as a challenge, rather than a threat. We should always look for the positive in any life situation, and see that if something occurs that makes us uncomfortable, it is a sure sign that we are being offered a learning experience. The more difficult the problem or the more uncomfortable you feel, the more important the lesson.

Cayce said that in particular, **"Worry and fear [are] the greatest foes to [a] normal healthy physical body . . . .."** (5497-1) Be especially careful of these two emotions. When you sense that you are feeling anxiety, try to find out what are the thoughts that are leading to these negative emotions. Reassure yourself that what is occurring in your life is for your own growth and is in your best interest, no matter how terrible a situation may seem.

Always try to fill your life with positive emotions by looking for the perfection in everything as it is, and remembering to enjoy life.

As Edgar Cayce said, **"Remember that a good laugh, an arousing even to . . . hilariousness, is good for the body, physically, mentally, and gives the opportunity for greater mental and spiritual awakening."** (2647-1) Cayce even went as far as telling one surgeon that he could help his patients more by arousing their hope, confidence, and faith, than through drugs or the scalpel.

We are the cause of our own illnesses. This was reiterated in several Edgar Cayce readings. One reading said, **"No fault, no hurt comes to self save that thou hast created in thine consciousness, in thine inner self, the cause."** (262-83) Another reads, **" . . . the weaknesses in the flesh are the scars of the soul!"** (275-19) Many people will blame a bacteria or a virus for their illness. Of course these organisms are the physical cause of some diseases, but they are attracted to us for a reason. All experiences are attracted to us by our Higher Self to restore balance in our body, mind, and spirit. By not taking proper care of our body we create physical imbalances that may cause our immune system to become weak. Then we become more susceptible to these predators.

Healing

Since Edgar Cayce gave more than 9,000 physical readings for some 6,000 people, he left a legacy of information that made his approach to healing very clear. His approach was a holistic one, meaning that each part of the body is influenced by the whole, and should not be treated without considering the rest as well. Of course, Cayce referred to the whole self as body, mind, and spirit, and his approach was much more than only physical.

Where doctors today treat only physical symptoms, Cayce recommended treatments to remove the underlying, usually non-physical cause. This is where the Cayce readings differed widely from traditional medicine in their approach to healing. For Cayce believed **" . . . healing of the physical without the change in the mental and spiritual aspects brings little real help to the individuals in the end."** (4016-1) A doctor may be able to relieve outer symptoms temporarily with drugs, but if the inner cause of the illness is not healed, it will keep returning until proper balance has been restored.

Healing to Cayce was spiritual in nature. In his words, healing requires the **" . . . attuning [of] each atom . . . to the divine that lies within each atom, each cell of the body."** (3384-2) Thus, he believed a person is healed when each atom of their body is in tune with their Higher Self, or the divine within. Also, he believed each cell to be important in its own right, saying, " . . . **every cell of the body is a universe in itself** . . . .." (1158-22) Each cell has its own consciousness, and must, in order for the body to remain healthy, function in harmony with the other cells and in union with the divine will of the entity.

Edgar Cayce also devoted many readings to interpreting the mysterious symbolism of the Book of Revelations. Surprisingly, he interpreted the entire work as symbolic of the attunement of self to the divine. His interpretation shows that the Revelation describes the process by which each cell of the body is transformed and brought into harmony with the divine will.

Cayce claimed that no matter what form of medical treatment a person receives, it all should be for the purpose of attuning to the divine. He said, **"And whether there is the application of foods, exercise, medicine, or even the knife, it is to bring the consciousness . . . of creative God forces."** (2696-1) Often the negative thoughts and emotions which cause us to be ill are rooted very strongly in our subconscious mind. We may have held for a very long time a harmful belief that is causing us to suffer physically. Louise L. Hay has written a wonderful book entitled *You Can Heal Your Life*. It contains a list of 300 common ailments with the corresponding negative belief and a positive affirmation one can use to change that belief. For example, for acne she gives as the probable cause, "Not accepting the self." "Dislike of the self." For the new thought pattern to counteract the harmful one, she gives, "I am a Divine expression of life." "I love and accept myself where I am right now."

The new thought patterns are only effective when they reach the level of the subconscious mind. The only way this can occur is if they are truly believed by the individual. Self hypnosis can be an effective tool in reprogramming the subconscious with more positive beliefs. Under an altered state of hypnosis one is in more direct contact with the subconscious, and it can receive programming more easily. I strongly recommend Henry Leo Bolduc's book, *Self Hypnosis—Creating Your Own Destiny*, for learning how to make your own self hypnosis cassette tapes that you can use to obtain changes in your subconscious and replace unwanted beliefs.

You also can incorporate the new thought pattern that Ms. Hay recommends into your meditation as an affirmation. During meditation we are reaching into our subconscious mind much as we are in hypnosis, so this technique also can be used very effectively. Simply repeat the affirmation several times to yourself while drifting off into a meditative state. Concentrate on nothing except this affirmation and really believe it as you are saying it. For remember, as Edgar Cayce said, " . . . **thoughts are things! and they have their effect upon individuals . . . just as physical as sticking a pin in the hand!**" (386-2)

When illness occurs, it is wise to seek treatment from some sort of healing practitioner. I do not suggest that we stop going to regular medical doctors, but I do think it is wise to consult with an expert in one of the many alternative therapies. Many remedies that conventional medical doctors prescribe, such as immunosuppressive drugs, tend to work against rather than with a body's own immune system. Although drugs may be effective in curing many illnesses, they are usually toxic to the body and contribute to a general debilitation of one's health. In fact, many drugs stay in the body long after they have served their purpose. They remain as poisonous deposits that pollute our body and tax our immune system.

The most effective medical treatments are those that work with the immune system and help to stimulate it. Edgar Cayce most often recommended spinal manipulations in the form of osteopathic adjustments to aid the immune system in healing the body. Osteopathy is a healing system very similar to chiropractic, in which a body's ability to be healed is enhanced by correcting any blockages in the nervous system that are impeding the proper response by the immune system. I personally use monthly visits to a chiropractor to help maintain my own health.

Another form of alternative healing I have also used with success is homeopathy. Homeopathy is a treatment that prescribes infinitesimal amounts of various herbs and other natural substances to stimulate the immune system. Usually, the remedy that is taken contains a substance that would produce similar symptoms to the treated disease if taken in large quantities. However, homeopathic remedies contain extremely minute amounts of the substance and are completely non-toxic. Yet the remedy, although very dilute, is sufficient to trigger the immune system to attack the problem. Ironically, the potency of a remedy is in direct proportion to its amount of dilution. In other words, a homeopathic remedy is made stronger by reducing the amount of active substance it contains.

Unfortunately, alternative healing systems such as osteopathy, chiropractic, and homeopathy, often do not provide immediate cures. People have become conditioned to expect a doctor to prescribe a miracle drug that will instantly alleviate one's symptoms. Although they are usually able to do this, often they have only eliminated the symptom and not the cause of the illness. Thus, many people suffer from illnesses that keep recurring, as the drugs that doctors prescribe become less effective.

Since alternative healing systems work with the immune system, they often take longer to see results. A chronic illness doesn't develop overnight. It takes a long period of negative thoughts or bodily neglect to weaken the immune system so that it can no longer maintain good health. Thus, sufficient time must be allowed for the immune system to be strengthened and to bring the body back into balance. The objective for permanent healing is to cure the cause of the disease, instead of only the symptoms. Unfortunately, the instant relief that most people are looking for, simply isn't to be found in alternative medicine, and as a result these treatments have been slow to catch on. Also, the American Medical Association (A.M.A.) has long been trying to discredit these healing systems, which it sees as obvious threats. After all, the drug industry is big business. The A.M.A. maintains control over the healing industry by successfully lobbying for laws that allow only licensed medical physicians, trained in conventional drug therapies, to diagnose or heal.

Spiritual Healing

The effectiveness of spiritual healing, also called faith healing, is becoming more recognized by the medical community. There have been many witnessed and validated cases of spiritual healing to prove its worthiness. However, most physicians believe that the person healed by these methods only gets well because of the placebo effect. Meaning, they believed they would be healed, so they were.

With spiritual healing, like all healing, the patient is the one responsible for the healing process. They are healed according to their ability to accept their own divine healing power, although they usually perceive it as the healer's power. Everyone has within them all that is necessary to restore and maintain balance in their body. However, most people don't truly believe this, or they would never be ill. When Jesus healed, he often said, *"Thy faith has made thee whole."* (Matthew 9:22) The faith he referred to is the amount of belief one has in the healing power of God. Because people believed Jesus to be a prophet from God, they had faith that they would be healed through him, and they were. Thus, through his own charisma, Jesus was able to bring a person's faith to the surface.

Cosmic Awareness has defined faith as, ". . . **the justified confidence in our capacity to understand who, in fact, we really are."** If we truly believe that we are divine beings, who carry God within us, then we know that we make our own reality. Once we understand this, we have the ability to heal ourselves. When Jesus healed, the healing was instantaneous. This is because the person was instantly transformed through direct contact with the divine love of the Christ Consciousness. Jesus was able to function as a channel for this healing energy. To complete our soul development on this plane we must bring the Christ Consciousness to our own awareness so we also may channel this energy and be brought into attunement with the divine within. Through this attunement we experience complete healing of our body, mind, and spirit. Standing between ourselves and this healing energy is our mind. The mind regulates the flow of this energy, and if our faith is small, the flow of this energy will also be small.

Awareness tells us that spiritual healing works on three basic principles:

1) Mind controls all bodily functions.
2) Mind can be controlled by suggestion.
3) Suggestion is the force that heals.

Our mind will allow our body to heal if we present it with positive suggestion in the power of faith. However, there are many blocks that prevent positive suggestions from affecting the mind. These negative attitudes are the result of the conditioning we have given our mind throughout our life. Some people, for example, have conditioned their mind to accept only those things that can be scientifically proven. Also, some people don't believe in their own immortality, and therefore won't accept anything of a spiritual nature. These are some unfortunate limiting ideas that block healing energy in many individuals.

We have already seen how positive suggestions can be programmed into the mind through hypnosis and affirmations. We have also seen that healing is the attunement of the body to the divine within, and that Jesus healed by bringing this to the consciousness of the individual according to their own faith, or their ability to accept the suggestion. Spiritual healing is therefore primarily about convincing a person's mind that it should allow the body to be made well through divine healing energy.

There are some psychic healers, most notably Alex Orbito of the Philippines, who use a technique known as psychic surgery. In this technique, the hands of the surgeon are plunged through the skin of the patient and enter the body without making any incisions. Blood clots and tissues containing negative energies are removed and discarded. This is all done while the patient is completely awake. Once the surgeon's hands are removed, the opening in the skin seals itself up instantly. This is a very impressive procedure and its effectiveness has been studied and corroborated by several medical doctors. However, as Alex Orbito will say himself, it is not physically necessary that his hands enter the body and remove tissues for it to be healed. The purpose of this procedure is to convince the patient's mind that something tangible and real is occurring. If a person sees themselves being operated on, they will believe that they are being healed because they have actual physical proof. Thus, by penetrating the physical body, the psychic surgeon is penetrating the mental blocks of the patient's mind, and clearing the path for the divine energy.

Spiritual energy flows into a person's body through the seven spiritual centers, known as chakras. Psychic, or spiritual healers, bring the patient's chakras into balance so the body can properly accept healing energy. The seven chakras are the points in the body where the spirit is joined to the physical. Each chakra is associated with a different region of the body. Any imbalance in the chakras will eventually manifest itself in the physical body.

Working from the bottom up, the first chakra is the root chakra located at the base of the spine, and it is associated with the gonads. The second chakra is located in the lower abdomen and is associated with the cells of Leydig or lyden. The third chakra is located at the solar plexus, between the rib cage and the navel, and is associated with the adrenal glands. The fourth chakra is the heart chakra and it is associated with the thymus gland. The fifth chakra is the throat chakra and is associated with the thyroid gland. The sixth chakra is the third eye, which is associated with the pituitary gland and is located in the center of the forehead. Finally, the seventh chakra is the crown chakra and it is associated with the pineal gland in the top of the head.

The chakras are also analogous to the seven levels of consciousness through which the four planes of self must develop. These stages of consciousness are the physical, emotional, mental, spiritual, higher mental, higher emotional, and the higher physical. They correspond to the seven chakras, from the root to the crown, respectively.

The chakras are the spiritual centers through which the life force energy finds expression. Each chakra corresponds to a different form of self expression. The attributes of each chakra are summarized in the table on the next page.

A psychic healer can sense the energies of each chakra and determine if an imbalance exists. A common technique used to balance the chakras and bring healing to the body is known as the laying on of hands, or therapeutic touch. This was spoken of by Jesus when he said, *"And these signs will accompany those who believe: in my name they will cast out demons; they will speak in new tongues; they will pick up serpents, and if they drink any deadly thing, it will not hurt them; they will lay their hands on the sick, and they will recover."* (Mark 16:17-18) Using the laying on of hands technique, the healer senses leaks of energy in the patient's aura by moving their hands around the body about an inch above the skin. The aura is an energy field that surrounds a person's body and is a manifestation of the spirit. The chakras are like vortices in the aura where the energy field is very concentrated.

	Endocrine Gland	Level of Consciousness	Expression
First Chakra	Gonads	Physical	Creative Energy
Second Chakra	Lyden	Emotional	Sexuality
Third Chakra	Adrenals	Mental	Inner Strength
Fourth Chakra	Thymus	Spiritual	Love
Fifth Chakra	Thyroid	Higher Mental	Communications
Sixth Chakra	Pituitary	Higher Emotional	Intuition
Seventh Chakra	Pineal	Higher Physical	Oneness with Divine

Usually when a leak is discovered in the aura the healer will sense a slight difference in temperature or a tingling sensation. After the leak is detected the healer then asks to be used as a channel for divine energy. The healer's hands are placed over the area and then the energy leak is repaired and the aura revitalized by the divine energy that flows through the healer and into the patient. With the energy restored the body can now more easily heal itself.

Some people use crystals to help magnify and focus the energy they are channeling. Crystals are receivers, amplifiers and storage cells of divine energy. When they are used in connection with spiritual healing, the flow of divine energy is often increased. Also, many people keep crystals with them wherever they go to help maintain a strong flow of energy into themselves.

Although the spiritual healing technique I have just described may seem difficult to some, let me assure you that it isn't. If you have a willing friend, it is an easy thing to try to sense their aura with your hands. Simply place your hands palms down about one inch above their skin, and move them slowly over their body, including their arms and legs. Try to notice any sensations you pick up in your hands. Don't be surprised if you feel something, and when you tell your friend about it they may admit to having some sort of pain or illness in that location.

An even easier technique that anyone can use to sense the aura is a swinging pendulum. I first learned this technique from Jean Munzer, director of the Metaphysical Center of New Jersey. To do this experiment, first you need to make a pendulum. For my pendulum I bought a piece of lead crystal about an inch long and tied it to a thread.

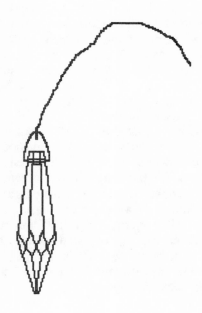

The Crystal Pendulum

After you've made your pendulum, try holding it over your friend's body. It should then start swinging in a circular direction to match the energy flow around the body. Move it around the body, and when the pendulum stops swinging in a circle, it means you have discovered an energy imbalance.

Another thing you can do is hold the pendulum directly over the chakras, one at a time. Now the pendulum should swing back and forth in a straight line over each chakra. However the direction of the swing should alternate when moving from one chakra to the next. If the pendulum starts to move in a circle it means that the chakra needs balancing.

There are some people who can see auras around a person. Edgar Cayce could do this so well that by just looking at a person he could give a diagnosis of their health problems and their emotional and mental stumbling blocks. Seeing auras is also not as difficult as it may sound, and it can be developed with practice. Try looking directly at a friend, or else at yourself in a mirror. Have them stand in front of a white wall or other light background. If you relax your eyes and imagine looking with your third eye in your forehead, you should start to see a white glow all around them, extending to about an inch above their skin. Keep practicing this technique and you may soon begin to perceive colors as well. There also are cassette tapes commercially available that can guide you through techniques to help you develop this ability.

To balance our own chakras we can again enlist the help of meditation. During meditation, you should try to visualize each chakra beginning with the root chakra and working up. Each chakra has a color associated with it and you should envision it emanating this color of light. The colors are red for the root chakra, orange for the second chakra, yellow for the third chakra, green for the fourth chakra, blue for the fifth chakra, indigo for the sixth chakra, and violet for the seventh chakra. You also should sense that each chakra is pulsating or spinning with energy. You can imagine a white light entering through your crown chakra and flowing down to each of your other chakras in turn, bringing them into alignment. If you need assistance, there are many cassette tapes on the market to guide you in a suitable visualization exercise.

Disease Prevention

Illness occurs on all levels: physical, emotional, mental, and spiritual. Thus to avoid disease we must maintain healthy attitudes and emotions, we should feel close to the divine within, and we must take proper care of our physical body. Perhaps the best way we can care for our body is to maintain a strong immune system. The immune system is greatly encumbered by accumulated waste matter, mucus, and accumulated toxic substances such as drugs. To strengthen our immune system there are two steps which need to be taken. The first is to purify the body of toxic obstructions, and the second is to keep it pure.

There is really only one effective method to purify one's body of all of the toxic substances and impure foods that have been ingested through the years. This method is fasting. Fasting is still a part of many Eastern religions today, and is mentioned frequently in the bible. It has also been reported that the messages of Mary, when she was appearing at Medjugorje, Yugoslavia, could be summarized as follows: prayer, conversion, fasting, penance, and peace. Thus, fasting may be an important ritual that few of us in the West observe. The reason it is prominent in religion, is because the people of the world have traditionally turned to their religion, or God, to know the best way to live on Earth. Most Americans believe that our scientific knowledge allows us to transcend such practices. However, as any scientist will tell you, the more you think you know, the more you discover what you don't know.

Fasting is important to our health because once we stop supplying our body with food, it immediately begins to eliminate waste. Every night while sleeping we are fasting and the body is beginning the elimination process. However, once you get up in the morning and begin eating again, the elimination cycle is ended. That is why it is generally a good idea to eliminate the habit of eating breakfast, or at least push it to as late in the morning as possible. By extending our fast, we extend the elimination cycle and rid the body of embedded toxins that are deposited deeper in our system. By occasionally fasting for a few days at a time we can clean out our system thoroughly.

Unfortunately, fasting is generally unpleasant for most of us. This is especially true if we have taken many drugs or medicines in the past. The residue from these will begin to come to the surface while fasting, and we could experience some nausea as a result. However, this is the price one must pay for polluting the body in the first place. If we don't eliminate these toxins by our own choice, they will eventually lead to illness.

Proper nutrition is vitally important to maintaining a pure, healthy, physical body. First, we must try to eat only the purest foods we can. So many of our foods are treated with pesticides and other chemicals that are toxic to our system. Although the Food and Drug Administration allows certain levels of these impurities in foods, the accumulation of these toxins in our bodies over periods of time weakens our system.

Second, the bulk of our diet should be fruits and vegetables. Edgar Cayce recommended that these should be eighty percent of what we eat. If we do eat meat at all, it should be limited to fish, fowl, or lamb. These are less dense than beef or pork, and therefore are more easily digested and assimilated.

Third, it is very important to drink plenty of pure water. Edgar Cayce and many others have recommended six to eight glasses a day. Water is important because it helps to flush the toxins out of our system.

Fourth, proper food combinations are important for proper digestion. Foods are either acid producing or alkaline producing in their chemistry. Meats and proteins are acidic, and require an alkaline environment in the stomach for their digestion. However, starches are alkaline and require an acidic environment for their digestion. If we eat both together we put the digestive glands in a rather precarious position, not knowing whether to make the gastric juices more acidic or more alkaline. Thus Cayce recommended that we don't eat meat or cheese together with starch, citrus fruit or juice together with cereal, or coffee with milk.

Finally, it is also important not to drink liquids with your meals. Liquids tend to dilute the gastric juices, and this obviously inhibits digestion. Wait at least twenty to thirty minutes after a meal before having anything to drink, to allow some time for digestion.

Besides fasting and proper nutrition it is also necessary that we give our bodies some good exercise. Exercise does not need to be strenuous, but it should provide increased circulation. Edgar Cayce has stated that " . . . the circulation, . . . is the main attribute to the physical body, or that which keeps life in the whole system, ..." (4614-1) Cayce and others have frequently recommended walking as one of the best exercises we can do. Massage is also very beneficial to stimulating the circulation. Also important are stretching exercises, such as those done in hatha yoga. I usually start my day with some stretching exercises, particularly head and neck exercises. I also do some twists and bends to limber up my back, and a few sit-ups and push-ups. I find this really helps to give me energy in the morning. It is also very important to breathe very deeply when exercising. Air contains our life energy, and proper deep breathing exercises are essential to maintaining peak vitality.

While on the subject of exercise, there is an interesting yoga posture that I found described in Jess Stearn's book, *Yoga, Youth, and Reincarnation*. I was formerly susceptible to sore throats and colds, particularly in the winter time. I have found, however, that if I feel a sore throat coming on I can often relieve it with the posture known as the Lion Pose. This is the main purpose for which it is commonly used. The pose, as given by Mr. Stearn, is this:

> Crouch down on heels, arms out straight and resting
> on knees. Tense whole body, extending fingers stiffly.

Roll eyes upward, tongue out and downward, and hold for
fifteen or twenty seconds.

If you feel a cold or sore throat coming on, try this two or three
times during the day. It may not be pretty, but it works. I believe it
stimulates and balances the throat chakra, promoting the release and
expression of pent-up emotions.

Besides walking and stretching exercises, spinal manipulations are
also very important. Besides treating disease, frequent osteopathic or
spinal manipulations and adjustments are a great preventative. They
keep the nervous system in order and maintain a good flow of
communication between the organs of the body and the brain. This is
crucial in maintaining a properly functioning immune system.

Finally, I recommend obtaining an astrological birth chart
interpreted by a competent astrologer. This chart can reveal the
tendencies you were born with which might lead to physical illness.
The sixth house of the zodiac is that which governs matters of health
and it is most likely where you will find reference to your inherent
physical weak points. It would be wise to be particularly mindful of
these parts of your body and to treat them with extra care. In addition,
a progressed chart is also a great tool. The progressed chart gives the
influences of the changing positions of the planets over time with
respect to their positions in your birth chart. Thus, a progressed chart
can tell when you are more likely to experience some form of illness.
This will give you the opportunity to take precautions such as choosing
your food more carefully, obtaining a spinal adjustment, taking
vitamins, or getting extra rest.

AIDS

I will conclude this chapter with a discussion of the recent plague
known as the AIDS virus. Fortunately, all I have said in this chapter
can be directly applied to AIDS. There are no incurable diseases. The
mind is the only true healer, and it can heal any condition in the body
as long as it is properly directed by the will. The first step in any
healing should be to try to identify a possible underlying psychological
imbalance that has attracted this disease and is manifesting in this form.
In the case of AIDS, we are looking for the reason that the spirit has
attracted the HIV virus to the body. If we consult the table in Louise
Hay's *You Can Heal Your Life*, we find that she lists as the probable
cause:

>Denial of the self. Sexual guilt. A strong belief in not being "good enough."

She gives as the new thought pattern to replace the old:

>I am a Divine, magnificent expression of life. I rejoice in my sexuality. I rejoice in all that I am. I love myself.

When one reviews the negative thought patterns given by Ms. Hay, it is clear why this disease is most common among homosexuals and drug addicts. A drug addict is attempting to escape from their life, so they are experiencing "denial of the self," while many homosexuals have guilt about their sexuality.

A person who is born with a body of one sex, but feels and behaves like the opposite sex, is most likely in continual inner conflict. Before a person is born they choose their parents and help to mold their own body into what would be suitable for their planned life experiences. Whatever the sex of the body, this is what was chosen by their spirit.

However, imbalanced conditions may occur in the physical body and in the mental attitudes which result in attraction toward one's own sex. Often sexual attitudes are carried over from previous lifetimes according to karmic law. A person's sexual attitudes are often a reflection of attitudes established in the past. For example, a person who once condemned homosexuals in a previous life may now be forced to face these same urges in themselves.

Another factor has to do with the transition from a body of one sex type in the entity's last lifetime to the opposite in this life. We are all inherently androgynous spirits. However we choose to experience the polarities of masculine and feminine energies that are necessary for creation. We choose to experience lifetimes as both men and women so as to experience both energy types. However, we may overemphasize experiencing a particular energy and repeatedly incarnate as either man or woman. This could make it difficult when we finally incarnate in the opposite sex again. For example, an entity who has been a man for several consecutive lifetimes may choose to be a woman in this life, but have the tendency to exhibit masculine behavior. This lifetime could serve as a transition point and in the next lifetime the entity could be more feminine and comfortable as a woman.

One way we can balance our masculine and feminine energies is through sexual relations with a partner of the opposite polarity. Certainly, sex is a physical act. However, it causes reactions on all planes of self. A person's attitudes toward themselves and their partner determine the extent of these reactions. Sex can be very important, as it balances these masculine and feminine energies within the individuals through direct exchanges. Together, two people neutralize the polarities of masculine and feminine, aggressive and passive, bringing both into a necessary balance and perhaps creating new life in the process. The balancing occurs on all levels, spiritual, mental, emotional, and physical.

Many of us create difficulties for ourselves in developing appropriate relationships to balance our sexual energies. Psychological imbalances from negative conditioning or experiences may lead us to become confused or guilty about our sexuality, and block our proper sexual expression.

The sexual urges are rooted in the lower self, particularly the second chakra. The physical urge for sex is found in this chakra. When we become sexually aroused, energy flows up our spine and stimulates our chakras. This energy is called kundaline energy, and it flows naturally during meditation and other spiritual work as well. Imbalances in the lower chakras, caused by mental attitudes toward sex, will block this energy from flowing beyond the lower self and reaching the higher chakras. For these people, sex is purely physical and does little to stimulate or balance them spiritually.

This condition manifests itself not only in sex, but in one's entire life and attitude toward spirituality and their Higher Self. It is difficult to raise one's consciousness to oneness with God when there is a block at the lower sexual level. Therefore, an individual of this type is truly one who is experiencing "denial of the self," meaning their conscious mind has not yet transcended the physical and recognized their own true nature as a Divine being.

Although not all homosexuals suffer psychological problems, there are many sources and causes of imbalances that can result in a person becoming homosexual. One is child molestation. Awareness discusses this possibility in the following reading:

> **This Awareness indicates that child molestation, or the threat or implication or desire to molestation, or the threat or implication of desire to molest one's child by a parent, step-parent, or parent figure is one of the major causes of homosexuality, particularly among women. This Awareness indicates that this appears to be related also to the attitudes of a mother toward her son; wherein the son feels a sexual attraction to the mother, but feels such guilt about the attraction that the entity is repelled by his own lust, or feelings which he considers lust. This Awareness indicates that this can create great problems for the entity, including that**

105

of homosexuality. (CAC 81-25)

Awareness has also stated that homosexuality is a result of obstacles in one's psycho-sexual development. The three phases of this development are the genital stage, the homosexual stage, and the heterosexual stage. The homosexual prolongs the homosexual stage because of stumbling blocks that have been laid in their psychological development. Sexual abuse at an early stage of one's sexual growth is an example of an experience that can create psychological blocks and imbalances.

Perhaps the most common stumbling block is one which results from repressed sexual energies. Sometimes one is conditioned by their parents or others to believe that sex is bad. They are taught to repress their sexual desires. As these energies build up, there is the need for them to be released. Those who are programmed against intercourse, perhaps through the fear of teenage pregnancy, may turn to relations with the opposite sex as an alternative.

Many psychologists suggest that homosexuals relieve their sexual guilt by accepting themselves as they are. This is necessary for everyone, for none of us have yet perfected ourselves. We are all here struggling to bring to balance our spiritual, mental, emotional, and physical selves. All of us can find something about ourselves that is imperfect. However, not only must we accept our shortcomings as they are, but we also must strive to correct them as we are able. There is no need for anyone to harbor guilt if they are determined to improve and grow. Guilt is an unhealthy attitude toward oneself that can only worsen the imbalances within.

A homosexual must accept themselves as they are, but they must recognize as well that they need to correct their sexual behavior by correcting their attitudes and redirecting them toward spiritual growth and development. Those who are in transition from past lives as the opposite sex, may be likely to develop psychological imbalances in this lifetime due to their uncertainty of their sexuality. These psychological imbalances have to be addressed before they can achieve inner peace and fulfillment with their sexuality.

By acknowledging our inner struggles we are able to begin the process of removing the blocks in our lower self, as we strive to integrate with our Higher Self. This requires accepting our own shortcomings and desiring to correct them. However, accepting oneself as a homosexual, and then believing that this is a desirable lifestyle, can be a mistake. Homosexuals must recognize that their sexual behavior is possibly a manifestation of an imbalance within which is prohibiting more balanced sexual relations.

Unfortunately, the increasing acceptance in society of homosexuality as a "natural" state is helping to create more homosexuals. This is stated by Awareness as follows:

> **This Awareness indicates that the problem in society in regard to the recent surfacing of homosexual situations is that it has become over-emphasized and given the feeling that it is natural and that entities should have a freedom of choice in terms of sexual preferences. The emphasis on this is such that it has caused entities who would not normally be homosexual to lean toward homosexual relationships simply because it appears to be the outrageous thing to do to strike back at society or at a particular representative of society. (CAC 84-16)**

Often many individuals, particularly women, become homosexual because they have had problems relating to men in their past. The acceptance of homosexuality in our society encourages them to give up on men and try women. Another problem is that since homosexuality is being treated as a normal, natural way of life, many people are beginning to believe that they are born homosexuals. They believe that because this is the way they were born, they cannot ever change. Present societal attitudes are stifling the growth of those who are stuck in their sexual development.

Homosexuals must not be condemned for being where they are in their development, but they should be encouraged to heal their imbalanced sexual attitudes and begin to seek more fulfilling relationships. Awareness addresses this issue of fulfillment in the following reading:

> **This Awareness indicates that it [homosexuality] is not the natural order of universal energies. It is not something which is to be seen as evil; it is simply something that is unfulfilling to those who are involved in this action in that although it may allow them many hours or months or years of gratification, they never will completely reach the depth of understanding that comes from a healthy relationship with a member of the opposite sex, and the souls of these beings will never have the fulfillment that comes from a fulfilling relationship with one of the opposite sex. (CAC 84-16)**

Today, many homosexuals are "coming out of the closet" in proudly declaring their allegiance to an "alternate life style." This is their way of countering the guilt that results from the rejection and condemnation by their peers and family members, in addition to the harsh judgements of society and the church. How ironic that many priests who are taught to condemn homosexuality find themselves struggling with these same urges. As Edgar Cayce once put it:

> **Condemn not, then that ye be not condemned. For indeed with what measure ye mete it will be measured to thee again. And that thou condemnest in another (yea, every man—every woman), that thou becomest in thine self!** (1089-3)

Sexual guilt is what attracts the AIDS virus. It also can be common in heterosexuals who have negative attitudes toward their own sexual behavior. This is why AIDS is not exclusively a homosexual disease. Many people are improperly conditioned by their parents while growing up, and taught that sex is bad. This is a mistake that must be rectified. For sex is an act that contains great healing power if it is properly utilized. Through sex we are brought into balance within and are able to manifest God's creative energy to produce a new physical vehicle for a human being.

The final belief that attracts the AIDs virus is that of "not being good enough." This belief is probably as equally common with drug addicts as it is with homosexuals. Both groups of people are suffering from low self esteem. Anyone who has AIDS needs to find ways to love themselves. They need to forgive themselves for their past, and begin anew. They must realize that all they have experienced has been for their own positive growth, and they must begin to see the perfection in that.

These new thought patterns, as I mentioned previously, could be seeded into the subconscious mind through affirmations and self-hypnosis. This is the most vital step to curing any disease. A person may end this painful experience if they simply choose to. This desire to be healed must be felt and believed not on just the conscious level, but deep in their inner self. Most importantly, the question must be asked, "Why did I bring this experience to me and what lesson do I need to learn from it?"

Ralph Duby, an interpreter of Cosmic Awareness, has given as the seven doctors of nature: fasting, air, water, sunshine, exercise, pure food, and mind. Awareness indicates that in the case of AIDS, air can be an effective doctor. A weak immune system, caused by the buildup of toxins due to improper diet, pollution, drugs, smoking, etc., is what creates susceptibility to any virus. Oxygen can counter viruses by strengthening one's immune system. Awareness states this in the following reading:

> This Awareness indicates that any physical body which is highly toxic in nature is low on oxygen. The cells do not contain sufficient oxygen because of the toxins in the cells, and this creates a healthy environment for viruses and illnesses, such as cancer, AIDS and other diseases. This Awareness indicates that in building up one's immunity system, the influx of oxygen into the body as that which can counter such things as AIDS and cancer and other diseases. (CAC 89-3)

To help cure many diseases such as AIDS and cancer, Awareness has recommended taking small amounts of dilute food-grade hydrogen peroxide in a glass of water. Hydrogen peroxide releases oxygen when it comes in contact with the blood, saliva, and bacteria. This helps oxygenate the cells of the body, and since these diseases cannot survive in a high oxygen environment, they are eliminated. However, Awareness cautions against the hazards of undergoing a treatment with hydrogen peroxide unless you really know what you are doing. In the appendix I list some sources Awareness has given to obtain food grade hydrogen peroxide and the proper instructions for its use.

Prevention is the best cure for any illness, and it is important that we maintain our immune systems in peak health. Remember, we are made up of body, mind, and spirit. Don't neglect any of them.

Prayer for Maintaining Good Health

Dear Lord, help us to ever be attuned to your Divine will. Help us to see your works in others around us as we channel your works as well. Bring balance to our body, mind, emotions, and spirit. Help us to greet each day with a positive light, knowing that your will is being done. Help us to recognize and accept your healing energy. Help us to remove the stumbling blocks we place in our way that prevent us from being made whole, and may we recognize our own ability to heal ourselves through faith. Thank you for the nutrients we receive each day that give us the energy to do your work. May we all eventually become attuned to your will and purpose, and be transformed by our oneness. Amen.

Meditation for Healing and Purification

To properly receive healing energy we must remove the physical, emotional, mental, and spiritual obstacles which impede the flow of this energy through our bodies. First, begin by relaxing your body from the top of your head, down to your toes. Next, visualize your body as a large vertical conduit, or pipe. Imagine that your consciousness is floating above this pipe, looking down into it. Now picture that ball of light in space again approaching you. See it beginning to illuminate you and everything around you as it approaches.

Imagine the ball of light slowly entering the top of the pipe at the top of your head. As it touches, feel your oneness with the Divine source. Feel how blessed you truly are to receive this healing energy. If you feel that there is any substance in the pipe near the top of your head that is impeding the movement of the light, imagine that the light is melting this substance away and making the pathway clear. Allow the light to proceed into your head. Feel how much your life is guided by this Divine energy, and how you are always being prepared to face new growth opportunities. Allow the light to dissolve any obstacles that you find here.

The light continues to drop lower into your body down into your throat, and now you sense your freedom to express yourself. What are you holding here that you have not been able to express before? Recognize your need to express your feelings to others and this expression can set you free from your anxiety.

110

Allow the light to dissolve any obstacles you find here and to continue down into your chest. Feel how much you are loved by God and how much you are deserving of love. Remember those friends and pets whom you love and who return your love unconditionally. The light dissolves any blocks here and continues to lower into your solar plexus region. Feel your power to overcome any obstacles and difficulties. Feel how this healing energy gives you strength. You are becoming superhuman because your body is being brought into perfect spiritual balance.

Dissolve any obstacles here, and allow the light to enter your lower abdomen. Feel your own sexuality and your desire to blend your own energies with another. Feel how wonderful it is to share deeply and intimately with another, gradually releasing your individuality and becoming one with another. If you feel any blocks here allow the light to dissolve them.

Finally, you allow the light to reach the base of your spine. Feel your personal creativity. What are you inspired to do or create in a unique and positive way? Sense those talents that are special to you. Imagine that you are putting these abilities into projects and plans that will serve the highest interest of yourself and others. Now the light is dissolving any few remaining obstacles at the base of your spine and the bottom of your conduit. Feel the ball of light become a steady stream of light flowing through you from the higher realms. Allow this energy to flow through you always, and stay in this state of awareness as long as you like.

CHAPTER SEVEN

Environment

Besides our own health, we also have a responsibility to maintain the health of our planet and all the creatures who live on it. God gave us dominion over the Earth, and we are its caretakers. However, we have been very poor custodians recently and our physical world is currently suffering from ill health. If there was a hospital for planets the Earth would be taken into the emergency room and its condition would be labeled "critical." I am sure most readers are now well aware of the tremendous damage that has been inflicted through air and water pollution, toxic wastes, chopping down forests, oil spills, etc.. The result of all this neglect is that the Earth's very existence is now threatened.

The Earth as a Living Being

What is this thing we call Earth? Is it just a chunk of rock and molten lava, or is it a living, breathing being? All New Age teachings agree that our planet is itself a living creature. Edgar Cayce put it this way:

> For, know all power, all influence that is of a creative nature is of the Father-God a manifestation. Not as an individual, not as a personality, but as good, as love, as law, as long-suffering, as patience, as brotherly love, as kindness, as gentleness; yet in all the beauties of nature—in the blush of the rose, in the baby's smile, in the song of the bird, in the ripple of the brook, in the wind, in the wave, in all of those

**influences or forces that bring to His creatures a
consciousness of Life itself and its awareness and its
activity in a material plane.** (1276-1)

Thus, all of creation, all of existence, material and spiritual, is of
God. Although the Earth does not possess a human personality, it is
nonetheless a manifestation of God's energy just as we all are. It also
has its own aura and energy field that must be kept in balance. The
Earth was created to teach us. Its purpose currently is to further the
development of humanity by providing a learning ground on which we
can manifest God's will in the physical plane. As our abuses cause the
Earth to crumble beneath our feet, it is only to make us aware of our
powers as co-creators and the responsibility that entails. Thus, it
currently is showing us the consequences of our actions that are not
in attunement with God's will and the forces of nature.

Life Force Energy

New Age philosophy teaches of a spiritual energy that flows through
us and permeates all of creation. The Hindus call this life-force energy
"prana." This energy exists in all things, and in actuality, matter is
nothing but a denser form of this energy. All things and all living
beings continuously receive this life energy from God, the Father, the
divine source.

An interesting characteristic of life-force energy is that we are all
channels for it. It enters our mind essentially unformed, but leaves it
impressed with the pattern of our thoughts. This is how we create what
are called thought-forms. Thought-forms are images or symbols that are
created from the life force energy by our thoughts. Many people who
can see auras claim that they see thought-forms in the auras of people
who have been thinking intensely about something. Other people, even
those who cannot see auras, may perceive these energies on a
subconscious level. The reactions and behavior of others toward you
may stem from a certain feeling derived from this perception. Thus,
your thoughts can truly create your reality.

Spiritual energy flows in a circuit and eventually comes back to us.
If you pattern spiritual energy with bad thoughts, then bad things are
bound to come back to you. This also is true for happy thoughts.
Cosmic Awareness gives this teaching in the Law of Gratitude which
states:

The Law of Gratitude is that sense of satisfaction where energy which has been given receives a certain reward. Energy which has been given moves out on that curved and unequal line, and when extended far enough, can only return to its source bearing gifts.

The Higher Self brings to us those things we ask for that are according to our highest good. Our thoughts pattern what we will receive. Through various experiences we learn that our thoughts and actions are important and have consequence. Our lesson is to experience how much more pleasant our life becomes when we are loving and caring in our thoughts and actions. Our life becomes blissful when we only occupy ourselves with those things that bring the most benefit to others.

The Earth responds to our thoughts in a similar manner, but on a larger scale. The condition of the Earth is a manifestation of our thoughts as a group, and is thus a reflection of the condition and soul development of our entire society. We are truly one with the planet as we are one with each another. We are beings of both earth and spirit. Our bodies are created from the matter of the Earth, and our spirits are connected to the Earth's spiritual energy.

As a vivid and personal illustration of this idea you can try a simple exercise for yourself. I was able to achieve amazing results the very first time I tried this. On a partly cloudy day, look to the sky and select a small cloud or group of clouds, preferably the white, puffy, cumulus type. Concentrate intensely on this particular cloud, noticing the other clouds that are near to it. Then begin dissolving the cloud by imagining a hot laser beam sweeping back and forth across it, heating the water droplets and evaporating them. Next, imagine a dry wind blowing away any remaining particles. After a few minutes you should notice this cloud disperse and then disappear. Finally, observe that the clouds that were near to this one have remained virtually unaffected. After I successfully did this exercise a few times consecutively without failure, I began to wonder if I was in some small way affecting the weather. With this question in my mind, I stopped dissolving clouds and I have not tried it again since.

"Natural Disasters"

When I first did the cloud dissolving exercise, I suddenly realized the awesome gift we are given in the ability to shape our world. With this gift, however, comes a great responsibility. Those who would in some way change our environment must first be certain of all the consequences of their actions. With this power to shape our environment with mere thoughts in mind, we can assume that the condition of the Earth is then a direct indication of the mental, emotional, and physical condition of its inhabitants. A Paul Solomon source reading made an interesting illustration of our connectedness with the planet with the example of AIDs:

> . . . the Earth's own system of immunal response, the Earth's own ability to heal itself, the sickness of Earth's own immune system, for you see the planet has AIDs . . . with the destruction of the ozone, for is this not that layer of protection that is meant to maintain the immune system of Earth to the forces, the destructive forces, of radiation of heat and the like, which upsets the natural balance of nature and climate control.

The planet is suffering from the same plague that is currently gripping humanity. Remember the Law of Correspondence that states, *"As it is above, so it is below . . . .."* Because of the planet's decaying immune system, we are inflicted with sudden climate changes and Earth shifts which result in what we call "natural disasters." These events are a result of the Earth trying to counteract the imbalances in its body caused by human neglect. They also serve to increase our sensitivity to the planet, and wake us up to our ignorance. As Spirit says, "As an agricultural society you once moved as the seasons, but now felt you have transcended such."

In 1989, a devastating hurricane struck the eastern coast of the United States and the Caribbean. Jamaica, the Cayman Islands, and Charleston were afflicted with tremendous damage totalling over six billion dollars. Cosmic Awareness sites this storm as an example of the changing weather patterns that are now occurring because of the Earth's imbalance:

> **This Awareness indicates that the recent hurricane, Hugo, as being the outgrowth of this changing weather pattern, especially because of the decreased ozone layer, and that such hurricanes will become more common as time passes, until the ozone layer is repaired, if it indeed ever is repaired.**

Awareness continues this reading by giving us a warning about the condition of the ozone layer:

> **This brings us to another consideration: It can take as much as 200 years to repair the ozone layer for the**

damage that has occurred within the past decade, if all further damage to the ozone layer is stopped immediately. If the ozone layer damage is continued further, it can reach a point whereby it simply begins to disappear on its own, regardless of whether there is an effort to reverse it or not, and in such case, the Earth itself then becomes a hothouse in which there is no relief. It will become or could become, much like the planet Venus. (CAC 90-1)

The prospect of our planet soon becoming inhabitable is a frightening one, and it is beginning now. This is not something that we can leave to future generations to worry about. As far as the actual timing goes, Awareness has foreseen that beginning in about thirty years we will all have to take special efforts just to remain healthy. The increased ultraviolet radiation is already affecting our health to the point where there are currently over 500,000 new cases of skin cancer diagnosed annually in the U.S..

We are not the only ones already feeling the effects, as many trees have been observed becoming burned and losing their needles because of the radiation. Just as oxygen is important to maintaining the immune systems of our bodies, it is vital for the Earth's immune system as well. Trees and plants are the source of our oxygen supply. This is well understood. Yet, in our greed we continue to cut down trees to make room for "progress." This is irresponsible behavior that clearly has no excuse. According to Awareness the diminishing of vegetation on the planet is an even greater cause of ozone depletion than fluorocarbons. Water pollution is also impacting the problem, since seaweed and underwater plants are another important source of oxygen. The way to solve the ozone problem is simple: plant trees instead of cutting them down, and stop polluting. Do it now!

Natural disasters are actually a blessing, much in the way of illness. Both serve to bring to our attention conditions of imbalance. The frequent hurricanes and earthquakes we have been experiencing are an example of events that force us to notice our environment and what we have done to it with our abuse and neglect. They also cause us to come together as a world community. When a serious earthquake or storm strikes, many nations around the world offer their aid. People send money and travel from all over to help rebuild the region. These positive community actions unfortunately only occur in times of calamity. The sooner the world as a whole realizes our responsibility for these events, when we stop polluting the air and water, when we stop destroying the rain forests, the sooner these disasters will subside.

IT'S TIME TO MAKE IT HAPPEN ON EARTH

Runaway Technology

Nearly everyone reading this book has probably noticed the staggering number of wild animals that are hit by cars and lie dead in the street everyday. This is another indication that we are living out of sync with nature. Man's technological expansion is gradually eliminating the natural habitats of most animals. As we develop more land into highways and condominiums we are leaving less space for the animals. Deer hunters often justify the necessity of their sport by claiming that overpopulation in the herds will eventually lead to many deer dying of starvation anyway. The reason the overpopulation exists in the first place is that we have virtually eliminated their natural predators and we have forced them to live in smaller areas that cannot support all of them. Because we have forced nature out of balance, hunters feel justified in killing.

Only our ignorance is to blame for our current predicament. Paul Solomon calls it, "technology in the hands of uninitiates." In other words, our technological advancement has exceeded our spiritual advancement, and we have experienced a technological evolution without a corresponding spiritual one. How ironic that those we consider the more "primitive" cultures, such as the American Indian tribes and the early eastern cultures, centuries ago realized our connection with the planet and our reliance upon it, while we are only coming to this realization now as it is forced upon us.

The Hopi Indians believe that in the beginning of this world there were two brothers: one white and one brown. The white brother was appointed to travel to far away lands in the east and use what he would find there to create new inventions. The brown brother was to remain in America and maintain a spiritual life at one with nature. After some time, the white brother was to return to the brown brother with his inventions. The brown brother would take the inventions and meditate on each to decide which should be kept and which should be destroyed. In this way, only those inventions of man that best served his spiritual ideals could be developed. The white brother got caught up in his inventions, however, and did not consult with his spiritual brother. As a result, many inventions dangerous to both the planet and humankind were developed and used.

This story symbolizes the way humanity has dismissed its spiritual side and focused on advances in material development. We have focused our energies on technological development unencumbered by the will of God and concerns for maintaining the balances of nature.

This story also symbolizes the nature of good and evil. Evil is the force that separates and drives humanity away from contact with its spiritual source and divine will. Through the temptations of material living we are driven increasingly further from this connection. It is time we begin to end evil on this world and return to recognition of our connection with the divine.

A misuse of technology is said to have caused the destruction of Atlantis. The Atlantean scientists, whose technology also exceeded their spirituality, were reportedly experimenting with a tremendous source of power derived from a crystal. Because of an error in their calculations, they ended up shattering the Earth's crust and triggering the Ice Age. This is frighteningly similar to our reckless use of nuclear energy, as exemplified by the accidents at Three Mile Island and Chernobyl.

There is nothing inherently wrong with technology. It can produce some glorious wonders for us. Because of our developments in communications and transportation, we have breached what were once considered vast distances and linked together the many nations of the world. Through these developments we have opened up pathways for the sharing of knowledge and resources among cultures.

However in developing vehicles for transportation, we selected for propulsion depletable petroleum products and a form of internal combustion that produces toxic gases as a waste product. In so doing, we began the cycle of taking energy from the Earth's crust and poisoning the Earth's atmosphere in return. Although we have been doing this for nearly a century, until now no one has thought of the harm this might be doing to the balances of nature.

Similarly, all of our modern communications equipment requires electricity. When Benjamin Franklin flew his kite in a lightning storm, he discovered electricity as it exists in nature. For man to produce it himself, he turned again to the way of fossil fuel and pollution. Soon after, nuclear fission was put into use and we began toying with powerful destructive forces that leave a toxic residue that remains radioactive for thousands of years.

Physics teaches us that every force or action has an equal and opposite reaction. Unfortunately, most scientists and engineers have chosen to ignore this principle when it applies to the elements and forces of nature. By filling the air with toxic fumes, we get in return acid rain. By exploding underground nuclear devices, we trigger sudden Earth changes. By chopping down trees and burning the rain forests, we get rapid climate changes. By destroying the ozone layer with aerosol propellants, we get exposed to dangerous levels of ultraviolet radiation.

Our major problem has been that when something new is discovered we rush to put it to use before it has been completely developed and all of the environmental impacts are known. Obviously, we began using nuclear energy long before all of the safety and waste management issues were addressed and understood. The only energy we know of today that is safe to use is that which comes from non-depletable, non-waste producing sources, such as solar power, water power, or wind power. The important lesson we must learn is that all of our technological advances must be carefully scrutinized before they are put into use. We should be certain to ask ourselves, "How does this invention help us accomplish our spiritual ideal of soul growth through love and concern for others?" "How does this invention impact the environment and the balances of nature?" If these questions cannot be answered in a positive sense, then perhaps we should revaluate the need for this invention.

Let us look at how the technological advancement we have achieved over the last 100 years has benefited us. In how many areas has technology been able to meet our spiritual objectives? Our major achievements have been in transportation, electricity, communications, medicine, space exploration, and, oh yes, military weaponry and surveillance.

First, most of our present technology is made possible with our advancements in electricity and electronics. Although many positive things are made possible with these technologies, the generation of electricity has proven to be a drain on our planet's resources and a major source of pollution.

Second, in the area of communications, we are now able to talk to virtually anyone, instantly, in any part of the world. We are also able to send television pictures wherever we like. The benefit to humanity is in a global sharing of knowledge and a linking together of all the separate civilizations of the world.

Third, in the area of transportation, we are not limited to only talking to people anywhere in the world, but we are able to go there with our physical bodies and with relative speed. Remember in biblical days most people spent days and weeks walking from one town to the next.

The advances in communications and transportation have shrunk the size of the world considerably for us. We no longer live in the dark about other people and places in other parts of the world. We have all but dried up the vast stretches of ocean that separate the continents from one another. We now have great knowledge about our fellow human beings across the globe. Although this is a positive development it has challenged our tolerance and acceptance of one another.

As the people of the world have begun to mix, we have become more aware of the differences between one culture and another. Our separateness and individuality have been violated by foreign influences. Many nations and people resent the changes in their culture that are occurring from intermingling with other nations. This has resulted in much prejudice and bigotry. Feelings of racial superiority have led to civil uprisings and attempts of conquest of one nation over another. I doubt if the inventors of our communications and transportation equipment ever realized the can of worms they were opening. Now that it's opened, however, we must move through these negative feelings of resentment toward one another and realize our oneness.

These inventions have greatly accelerated our discovery and knowledge of other cultures. However, this has come with a very high price. The burning of fossil and other fuels to power those inventions has polluted our atmosphere. In return, we suffer from increased incidents of lung disorders. I believe that advances in transportation and communications have had great benefits for humanity. However, we have rushed into using these technologies before we could discover a safer, cleaner way of implementing them.

Fourth, we have made advances in medicine that have enabled us to lengthen our life span and cure many formally terminal diseases. But did you ever notice that for every disease we develop a cure for, a new one seems to develop to replace it? Maybe we have won some battles, but we are far from winning the war. Medicine will never eliminate death and disease while the need for them remains. The purpose for illness is to bring to our consciousness those areas of imbalance in our psyche. As long as we continue to live our lives without being attuned to the divine will of God, disease will exist. Why are we spending so much effort on developing new drugs and surgeries, and so little on the real cause of disease?

Fifth, many people are scratching their heads lately for a possible benefit to space exploration. Perhaps the whole thing is driven by our instinctive curiosity. Since we have learned to travel over the Earth to discover what lies beyond our shores, we now seek to know what lies beyond our planet. However, God gives us everything we need to accomplish our purpose right here on Earth. That which lies beyond the planet we are not ready to experience. The development of humanity must reach a more evolved state before we begin scattering ourselves among the stars. What lies beyond our own planet cannot help us until we begin to help ourselves. Our journeying must begin with the journey inside ourselves. Focusing our attention on worlds outside our own, will only distract and confuse us. Humanity must be united in oneness before we begin to intermingle with other life forms. Otherwise, we may find that we will fragment ourselves across galaxies and lose our identity as humans.

Finally, the advancement in military weaponry has been staggering. We now have the ability to destroy the world countless times over simply by pushing a button. Amazing! With all the satellites orbiting the Earth, and their sophisticated cameras, we can spy on our neighbor and find out what he's not telling us. There is no way I can justify the tremendous expense of creative talent on military technology. Our distrust and fear of one another has caused us to enter an arms race to maintain national security through the threat of mutual destruction. Our fear and hatred is what motivates us in military advancement. This is a clear sign of our spiritual ignorance and immaturity. These negative attitudes toward others are only reinforced by building weapons to kill one another. This is contrary to our true purpose of loving and helping one another through recognition of our oneness.

When viewed in this light, what have we really accomplished with our material technology? How many of our inventions do you think our Hopi brothers would say we should keep? Perhaps our efforts would be better spent in moving toward recognition of our spiritual purpose and union with God and all of creation. This can be thought of as development of a spiritual technology to meet our spiritual needs, rather than a material one.

Spiritual Technology

Perhaps when our spiritual development catches up with our technological development, we'll realize we already have all the power and tools we need right inside ourselves. A natural benefit of spiritual awareness is the development of our own personal power in the form of psychic gifts. These include such phenomena as telepathy, clairvoyance, clairaudience, auric sight, psychometry, and psychic healing.

Edgar Cayce claimed that we all can do these things but we have forgotten how, just as we have forgotten our spiritual purpose. When we begin to recognize our spiritual selves, we experience how much more power we possess inside ourselves than we could ever create from matter. Through recognition of our spiritual bodies we are able to use senses of perception that we have forgotten we possess. These are known as the astral senses and are a part of everyone's spiritual body. Through these senses we are able to see, hear, touch, taste, smell and know more than we could ever obtain physically. I have personally experienced the unfoldment of some of these senses in myself and my life is increasingly enriched as I am able to use these to help others.

By perfecting our oneness with God and creation, as Jesus did, we are able to perform the great works that he did in the name of God. Remember Jesus said *"Truly, truly, I say to you, he who believes in me will also do the works that I do; and greater works than these will he do, because I go to the Father . . . .."* (John 14:6-12) Thus, our true destiny must depend more heavily upon the advancement of a spiritual technology than a material one.

Jesus served as an example of what we might be able to achieve. All the things he did, he did so we may witness the boundless powers of God working through a man. Perhaps we have not yet learned the great lesson he came to teach us by example: When one attunes themselves to the will of the Father, all things are possible.

Although this is not the path humanity as a whole has pursued, some people over the course of history have. For example, there have been many yogis in India who have been able to perform astounding feats. These include full use of all the psychic faculties, in addition to levitation, bi-location, and teleportation. They have overcome the limitations of the physical body by surrendering their will to God. Many yogis are reportedly able to transport themselves anywhere instantly. Some are able to be at two places simultaneously. They are able to send their thoughts anywhere without a device of any kind. They are healed almost instantly of any injury or illness. They travel through space beyond our planet, beyond our solar system, beyond our galaxy, by projecting themselves out of their bodies. For a fascinating account of just a few of these people, please read *Autobiography of a Yogi* by Paramahansa Yogananda. In this book, Sri Yogananda relates the ecstasy of experiencing life on the spiritual path.

Our emphasis on progress must now shift from a material one to a spiritual one, with the development of spiritual technology. By spiritual technology I mean less concern for the direct material accomplishments and more emphasis on spiritual evolution. For instance, we can improve our communications by using existing, but latent, psychic abilities of telepathy. We can travel vast distances in an instant. We can travel through the Earth, above it and out into the solar system, into other solar systems and galaxies, by simply leaving behind the security and familiarity of our bodies. We can satisfy our curiosity and need to explore what lies beyond by looking into the universe within ourselves. This was put most beautifully by Pretty Flower, an entity channeled by Eileen Rota, as, "The longing to be in the great, wonderful universe would be the longing to journey deep within our beings."

These abilities are the next step in the evolution of humanity. A

Paul Solomon reading even went as far as predicting that we would soon begin to develop a third lobe of the brain that will join together the two hemispheres we have already, greatly helping us to develop our psychic potentials.

Saving Our Planet

Now that we have ventured so far off the spiritual path, we are beginning to realize the dire consequences this may have. Not only are we faced with the destruction of our planet, but also ourselves. In the coming years as we experience global warming and increased levels of ultraviolet radiation, many catastrophic events will be triggered. For instance, scientists are worried that the polar ice caps may begin melting. This would dramatically increase the water level of our oceans, and flood out many coastal communities. We are already experiencing an increase in the frequency of earthquakes. Shifts in climate will likely result in severe droughts and floods. These things will be increasing in frequency and severity as we reap the Earth's reaction to our reckless actions.

However these events, although tragic and deadly, carry a very noble purpose. They will force us to wake up to our ignorance. They will unite us in an effort to end the pollution and the destruction of our forests. This has already begun as more people speak out. However, political and economic concerns are still interfering with the immediate action that is necessary. Because of the big business lobby groups, our government is far more concerned by the economy then the environment.

It is time that our spiritual development must catch up to our technological development. We must change our priorities to make our environment a chief focus of our attention. Perhaps now we can begin to put inventions and knowledge to work to save the planet. It is time that we use our technology to express our love toward our planet instead of satisfying our personal greed. This is a call for us all to contribute toward repairing the damage we have done. To find out what we as individuals can do please read the book *50 Simple Things You Can Do To Save The Earth*, by the Earthworks Group. I have supplied their address in the appendix. Remember if you don't do it, then who else will?

Prayer to Heal the Earth

Dear Lord, we ask that you guide us to live in balance and harmony with all your creations. We ask that all we do and all we seek to create, be according to your will. Lord, we ask that you help us to realize the consequences of living out of attunement with your will and that you help us to repair the damage that our previous ignorance has caused. We thank you for providing the Earth as the perfect teacher and learning environment for our lessons. Help us to find your divine love within ourselves and direct it toward one another and the planet. Amen.

Meditation to Heal the Earth:
A channeled message from Gaea,
the spirit energy of Mother Earth

Begin this meditation by perhaps focusing upon some form of nature that you have near you at this time. Perhaps a flower, or a plant, or a tree, or something that is near you that represents nature and the creations of the Earth. Perhaps you may choose to sit outside on the Earth to better feel its energy during this meditation or perhaps you may just envision that you are doing so. Envision that you are in a garden or park of some type that contains many of the natural wonders, many of the natural beauties and sights that are the consequence of the work of this planet.

Now that you have this before you, imagine that you see a glow around the plant or other object you have chosen. Imagine that you see the energy that is in this and that you see the aura of this. See how alive this plant or flower is. See how it seems to vibrate and move the energy around it. Focus on this energy and now see the energy that surrounds your own body, and see that it is of the same substance. It has the same glow, the same vibrant energy. And now, reach out and touch this object. Feel the energy link between yourself and the flower. Feel how now you have become one with this, as the energy is common between the both of you, as it surrounds the both of you without a separation between you.

Now allow yourself to expand your focus. See how the energy of this plant also touches and makes up a part of the energy which surrounds the entire Earth. See how the Earth is surrounded with a white glow of divine energy, and how vibrant and alive it truly is, for it is the total of the energy of all the creations on this planet. For all are of the energy of this planet. For nothing comes into this world without coming from and through the energy of this planet. See how you all make up a piece of this energy which surrounds the world. See how you are all swimming in this ocean of energy, and that your own energy is a small but important part of the whole.

Now imagine that you would like to increase the energy of this planet. You would like to increase the positive energy to help balance out the negative energy that has been brought by all of those deeds and actions that were not in the best interest of, or in the harmony with, the balances of the energy of nature and the planet. Take your time to fill yourself with that golden white light. Feel it growing from within you, a ball that grows and vibrates with energy.

Now feel it growing and growing, and as it is growing so are you getting larger and larger, growing and growing so large that now you are bigger than the planet and you are holding it in your hands. If you wish, you may hold a globe in your hands at this time to help you better visualize this meditation. Hold the Earth in your left hand and raise your right hand to the heavens and ask in your heart that you be given healing energy to give to this planet. Continue to hold the Earth in your left hand, and receive the energy, the golden white light, in through the fingertips of your right hand. Feel it enter. Feel it grow inside you as it enters and is stored inside you. Now take your hand and place it over the globe, over the top end so it is opposite that of your left hand. Feel the energy pass between your hands. See how the energy penetrates and goes through the Earth and around it, and fills it with energy and light. See how bright the Earth is becoming and how much more alive it is. Now wave your hand over the Earth and imagine that you are balancing out those points of negative energy with positive energy. Wave it over and balance the energies of the planet. Do this for as long as you like. We feel and receive the energy you are giving us, and we thank you for it. We ask that you continue to feed us with your positive enerby and to discontinue feeding us with your negative energy.

CHAPTER EIGHT

Business

All of life is a business. In business, we put out to get back. In life we do the same. Any energy we shape and channel into this world returns to us "along that curved and unequal line," as Cosmic Awareness has stated. All of life is an exchange of energies between ourselves and our environment. It is how we know we exist. Thus, life is business, and business is life. Because of this, spiritual principles apply very directly to the world of business. The Law of Karma, the Law of Gratitude, and the Law of Prosperity are just a few that are very important in business relationships. Just as we can apply them to our lives to bring us peace, love, and prosperity, so must we also apply these in our businesses. However, most business people don't consciously recognize these principles. As a result, our economy often experiences times of struggle and hardship.

These struggles, like problems in all areas of life, are for our own growth and show us how we have separated ourselves from our divinity. They show us that real success and happiness occur when we learn to incorporate spiritual guidance and oneness to our everyday affairs.

The problems of American businesses are growing and becoming more apparent. American companies are increasingly losing much of their market share to foreign competition and the nation is facing fiscal crisis. The U.S. trade deficit has exceeded 130 billion, while our country's debt tops four trillion dollars and continues to climb.

Free Enterprise and the Nature of Competition

There are several reasons that people give for slow economic times. Most analysts point to external reasons such as oil prices and foreign competition. But these are not the causes of our problems. The failure to adapt to these changing conditions is what truly is behind the downfall. The Law of Change is a universal law and it is described by Cosmic Awareness as follows:

> **There is a Law which governs all things and allows no thing to remain unchecked, and allows no checks to remain unchanged. That in anything seen, done, experienced or known, you may look at it and say with absolute certainty: "This, too, will pass."**

The Law of Change is a necessary principle for our spiritual development. It keeps us from becoming too comfortable and lazy. It challenges us with ever changing conditions and experiences, pushing us onward toward movement and growth.

Change is inevitable, and relying on old principles which no longer work under a changing business environment is akin to committing fiscal suicide. The tendency of American management has been to rely on the techniques that once brought us great success and made us into a superpower nation. However, clinging to these antiquated policies has brought the Law of Change crashing upon us as we suddenly realize we are no longer the number one economic power in the world. Management skills in American businesses are still in the dark ages. Today's businesses are just now realizing that the old management style of the World War II era is no longer effective with the modern generation of workers.

America has lost its economic supremacy to the Law of Change. Other countries, such as Japan, continue to grow economically, while the U.S. continues to slip. Soon our situation may become so severe that we will have no choice but to reform and restructure our businesses and national economy. A disturbing consequence of our economic decline has been the large amount of foreign investors buying up much of our properties and businesses. Their willingness to pay extraordinarily high prices for American land, buildings, and companies, is pushing up their prices. Cosmic Awareness recently gave us this warning:

> **The time may come when many of the natives of the U.S., the American citizens will find themselves being priced out of a market that is dominated by foreign investors, foreign buyers, so that the lands, the homes, the buildings are beyond their reach.** (CAC 90-1)

The ability to own a home, to start a business, and to prosper according to one's deeds, are the key elements of the American dream.

As fewer of us are able to realize this dream, we are drawing closer to our economic rock bottom.

Japan and other foreign competitors are teaching the United States a lesson about free enterprise. For decades, American business has been based upon the principle of competition: only the fittest survive. The focus of management has been more on destroying the competition through advertising and marketing, than on creating a quality product. The threat of competition has overwhelmed the consciousness of business owners and the commitment to quality and excellence has become secondary. There is an inherent fear that another's success somehow limits our own. It does not bode well karmically for a person or company if the only way they can succeed is by helping another to fail.

Many business owners believe that their available market size is limited by the number of competitors. What people have to realize is that the market is always large enough to support a truly quality product no matter how many competitors there are. When a company can offer a consumer exactly what they want at a reasonable price, they will be successful. Their continued success depends upon their ability to adapt to changing consumer needs, while continuing to produce quality. Therefore, the focus of a successful business is not on the competition, but on meeting the wishes and needs of the consumer.

To overcome this competition-driven survival instinct, businesses need to begin working together. To solve the economic problems companies need to band together and make business success a cooperative venture. Competitors must now become partners in restoring quality and excellence to their products and rebuilding the economy. Many companies keep much of their research and development proprietary. These secrets are usually well kept from companies in this country. However, foreign companies usually have little difficulty copying this technology once the product becomes available to the public. Once they do, they usually develop a product that is a close replica and costs a fraction of the price. Because of trade secrecy, American companies waste much time and effort in duplicating one another's research. Greater sharing of technology must occur if America is to regain its business strength. By eliminating redundant research, companies will be able to run more efficiently and move ahead more quickly on new products. Once we tear down the trade barriers that exist between our own companies, we will be able to tear down the barriers between ourselves and foreign companies. Finally, we should integrate into a global economy based on trust and cooperation between all businesses.

Many people fear that when companies begin working together, prices will go up because the competition element has been eliminated. However, in actuality, only the threat of competition appearing is enough to keep companies from charging unfair prices for their goods. If a company or group of companies monopolizes a market and they raise the price of their product too high, this will invite others to start a similar business and sell their product for a lot less. Thus, the competition will return and their market share will decrease. Thus, businesses who do not charge fair prices will immediately recognize that they cannot remain successful for long.

No one but ourselves can take away our success. There is no limit to how successful one may be regardless of competition. Success is not made by eliminating the competition. It is made by individuals doing their life's work according to their spiritual ideal and giving it all their energy. One who is successful is one who has found their life's work and are doing it.

Finding Your Life's Work

The first step to discovering your life's work is to formulate a spiritual ideal. This ideal should begin with what you would like to accomplish on a spiritual level in this lifetime. Remember, we are all here to develop spiritually and this is our primary purpose. This is a personal quest, but your spiritual ideal should in some way involve service to others. This is because it is only through service to others that we can grow in our spirituality. Formulate your spiritual ideal as if there are no limits to what you can do. For this first step, disregard how you will accomplish your ideal. Just think of the highest purpose your life can have without placing any limits on it, and make that your spiritual ideal.

As I said in other chapters, your life's work usually involves using your God-given talents. Thus, the second step to finding your life's work is to discover what these talents are. This is usually not very difficult. Most people know what they are really good at and what they enjoy doing. However, many people forget to recognize certain talents because they lack self confidence or they don't feel they could make them into a worthwhile career. Make a list. Begin the list with your spiritual ideal, and then under that write down all the things that you are presently good at doing. Then, under that include all of the things that you are interested in and the skills you would like to develop. Put down all those things you spend your leisure time doing. What do you like to read about, or what interests you on TV?

Now, with this list completed you can take the third step, which is to formulate a specific plan. Look at your list and try to think about how you can use each of these items to accomplish your spiritual ideal. First look at the ones you can already do now. Then consider the ones that you may not be ready for now, but which you may be able to develop with the proper training or study. Meditate on these ideas and let the inspiration come to you. Don't let money concerns or family obligations enter this process. Believe that you can be successful at whatever you choose. If you choose what is truly right for you, then your Higher Self will always bring to you an abundance of whatever you need.

Finally, the last step is to begin your life's work. Since you now have identified what you would like to accomplish, and what you will do to get there, the only thing left is to go!

Plan to proceed one step at a time. If you don't feel good about your present career, don't necessarily quit your present job or close your present business until you are already successful with your new one. You may need to continue with the work you have already begun while you are beginning your new venture to make the transition as smooth as possible. For instance, it may not be wise to give up your present income, when you still have many debts to pay, until you are sure that your new work will be lucrative enough to cover these. Be cautious, but definitely don't remain stagnant. Since what you will be doing will be your life's work, you will have tremendous self-motivation. This will be a true sign that you are now definitely on the right track. Things should come easily to you, because this is what you were meant to do. Also, if you can find a good psychic it may be worthwhile to see if you can get confirmation from them that you have truly found your life's work. A good psychic will be able to tap into your Higher Self and get this verification. They also can be helpful in identifying your talents. Astrology is especially good for uncovering latent abilities.

Any business will be successful if it is founded on a spiritual ideal. If an entrepreneur begins a business to accomplish their life's work, then it will be successful if it is truly in their highest good. We must eliminate the limits we have placed on ourselves by believing that competition can hurt us. There is an excellent book by Sanaya Roman and Duane Packer entitled *Creating Money—Keys to Abundance*, that discusses our limiting beliefs and how we can transform them. They give several visualization exercises that help you to believe in your success and then manifest it. In one section they discuss competition as follows:

If you are competing with other job applicants for a job, or other businesses for a client, or wanting to get a grant or funding, do not view yourself as competing with others. If it is for your highest good to get the money, client, or job, you will.

It is true that whatever comes to you is for your highest good. This also means that your business may not always prosper. When you lose touch with your spiritual ideal, or when you have completed a certain phase of your development and it is time to move on, your Higher Self will let you know. Things will become increasingly difficult and success formulae that used to work will no longer be effective. It is then time to revaluate your ideal to see if maybe it has now changed. Maybe now you can do even greater good than you have done in the past, and it is time to open to new opportunities.

When a business suffers a bad period, it is because there is something that must be learned. Just like with individuals, every struggle is an opportunity for growth. Competitors can be a blessing if they show you your mistakes. God bless the Japanese! They have shown businesses in this country that they can no longer be successful with the old ways. Businesses must grow on an inner level to recognize their own highest ideal, and to recognize the value of each person in the company. American businesses have for the most part been motivated solely by profit. It is time that they aim for a higher source for their motivation. It's time for a change.

Restructuring the Work Environment

The true nature of business is creation. As divine beings, we are natural co-creators of our world. Business is the avenue through which we may bring our creative ideas into manifestation and receive a reward for our accomplishments. We recognize a need for a product or service for others and then we fulfill this need. This is the main function of business and it should not be forgotten. It is just as necessary for a business to have a spiritual ideal as it is for a person. This ideal should ultimately be to enrich the lives of all who come into contact with the business and product by supporting their highest creative abilities. Employees must all be considered inventors. In any company, whether it is the engineer, the secretary, the assembler, or the bookkeeper, everyone should have the opportunity to create, and be rewarded for it. They may not all be able to create the company's newest high tech widget, but they all can develop new ways of doing their own jobs better. After all, this is their personal field of expertise.

To be creative is to be in touch with one's Higher Self. Since we each possess a Higher Self that is connected to the universal consciousness, we are all capable of more creativity than we realize. Our personal creative ability is directly related to how well we can attune our conscious mind to the Higher Self. Efforts to link with the Higher Self must be encouraged in each company member if the fullest potential of the individual and the company are to be realized.

The spiritual ideal of the company should be reflected in the product or service. Every business should concentrate on providing a product or service that assists the consumer's ability to be their best, most creative and positive self. Any business that does this will have the enormous resources of divine energy behind them to bring to them whatever they need to succeed. To formulate this business spiritual ideal and determine the best product or service for them to provide, it is necessary for the owners of the business to be in touch with their own Higher Selves. First, they must be certain that what they are doing is in harmony with their own personal spiritual ideal. After this point is reached, it is then necessary for them to hire only employees whose own spiritual ideals blend with that of the company.

It is also important for a manager of a business to be certain that the employees are placed in the job that is most in attunement with their higher ideals. In other words, a manager should be aware of a person who is not in the correct job and is not making best use of their inherent talents. A manager must be doing what he loves to do, and must be certain that his employees are doing the same. Thus, an important function of any business should be to help each person identify their ideal and work toward it. When every employee is working out of motivation from their Higher Self, they will be like an indestructible army. They will all be synchronized and attuned on an inner level, so there will be no room for confusion. Teamwork is a great lesson that can be learned in the business environment. Learning to work closely with others toward common objectives is one of the most important areas of personal growth.

If some employees are not in attunement with the business ideal, it is best not to keep them around. It is not in their highest good, nor in the company's, if they continue to struggle to channel their energies where they don't belong. However, some employees may simply be in the wrong job, but still in the right company. With these people it is best to encourage them to pursue a function that best uses their inherent talents. For example, an accountant with great artistic abilities may be more content in the graphics or advertising department. It is important to identify those employees who may have made a career choice in

133

the past that does not suit them in the present. They should be encouraged to get whatever training they may need to change their career so that they can better serve themselves and the customers of the company.

There is another important point that should not be overlooked. As part of our development we all must learn to be content wherever we may be. It is not right for us to dislike anything. We must realize that whatever situation we are in is for our own benefit, and that we will not be freed from any circumstance until we learn the lessons involved. Again, we must recognize our oneness with everyone and everything. Everything in our lives is an extension of our own selves. Any form of hate or discontent is an imbalance. Sanaya Roman and Duane Packer describe this principle as follows:

> The more you dislike your business, the longer you may be in it. One of the principles of your universe is that every situation in your life is teaching you how to love. You cannot leave something until you love it. You are tied to things you don't like.

We must learn to love everyone and everything as we love ourselves. All is the way it is in our lives for an important reason. Any imbalance is balanced as we learn from our mistakes. Thus, in order for a person to make a change in their business or career, it first may be necessary for them to learn to love their present job. Otherwise they may just find the same dissatisfaction wherever they go. This can be easily accomplished once it is realized that this career or business, whether they like or dislike it, is an important learning experience.

Take time to think about all the constructive lessons you may be experiencing while at your present job. Definitely do not overlook your personal relationships with co-workers. The people you work with are the most important elements of any job. Thank the universe and your Higher Self for the important growth experiences you have had through your work. Through the recognition of all your job has taught you, perhaps you can learn to like even a job you once hated.

Personally, I have been somewhat dissatisfied with my career in engineering for the past six or seven years. This feeling intensified when I began to become interested in metaphysics. I found that I detested the materialistic motivations and the lack of a common ideal I found in any job that I took. I began to search frantically for another career I could enter, but nothing at the time seemed right. However, I felt this strong underlying pull toward metaphysics, and I knew I wanted to spend more time learning and teaching about these subjects. Then I read the above passage from *Creating Money*, and I asked myself what I was learning from my career in engineering. The answer came to me that I was obtaining a firm grounding in the material world, as a preparation for my spiritual work to follow. I discovered that I was living a life of balance between the material and the spiritual, rather than foregoing the material and only focusing on the spiritual. I realized that my purpose was to apply spiritual principles to material living and bring the two into harmony. If I had left my job to pursue my spiritual growth full time, I may not have learned how to blend a spiritual life with a material one, and my spiritual growth may have actually been hampered.

My own life then began to make more sense to me, and my path became more clear. I had learned a very important lesson. This is to find the perfection in everything, because it really is there. Dissatisfaction only breeds negative energy that keeps you stuck in one place until you remove it. Negativity blocks the flow of the positive creative energy that brings happiness and clarity.

The Business of Karma

Edgar Cayce once gave a reading that stated:

> **Also know that what ye sow, in mental, material and physical relationships, will be measured back to thee again. This should be the basis of thy policies, of thy attitudes, of thy dealings with others.** (1634-1)

Certainly our business lives are the focus of much of our material physical relationships and our dealings with others. We incur karma in all of our activities. It is important that we realize we cannot live a spiritual life at home and be deceitful and uncaring at work.

Businesses, although often treated by the law as separate entities, are nothing more than a group of people. When the people running a business allow their company to pollute the environment or cheat the public, they are incurring negative karma. This karma will return to them as well as their business. Karma may be incurred by businesses through false or misleading advertising, through faulty or low quality products, or through the creation of toxic byproducts, to name a few. A business that does these things will find success to be much more difficult. A day of reckoning will come when they will not get the contracts they should, their products will not sell well, and it will feel as if someone is out to get them. Indeed this is true, for the results of their own misdeeds are returning to get them.

People often tend to dissociate themselves from their jobs or their businesses. This is a grave mistake, for whatever one does in the name of business they also do to themselves. Big business is subservient to us, not the other way around. We are the creators that give life to businesses, and we can easily take it away. We are responsible for all that our business does, and we will incur its karma.

There is, of course, much positive influence that can come from business. As one example, business has great influence upon world peace. When business is conducted on a worldwide level, and there is free exchange between countries, it helps to remove the artificial barriers between them. Countries cooperate to a greater extent, concerned that disagreement between them will impact them economically. The success gained when businesses and countries work together proves that the greater gain is in harmony and agreement. Cosmic Awareness recently made this statement regarding the Cold War:

> **. . . the way to diminish the potential for nuclear war was through commercial interchange between Russia and the U.S., for when business is invested in so-called enemy country, these businessmen have great influence in their respective countries, and this can help to prevent the warring attitude and atmosphere.** (CAC 90-1)

Because of the great increase in world trade in recent years, we are moving closer to the reality of a single world community. Business is paving the way for greater cooperation between nations, as they depend more upon trade with one another. Energy is exchanged between countries in the form of goods and services. This exchange has the power to break down the walls that separate us. It is what will soon lead us to a single world government based upon human need instead of human greed. But this will only occur when our spiritual development is advanced enough so that everyone recognizes their oneness.

Intuitive Decision Making

Ask any manager what they get paid to do, and they'll likely tell you it's to make decisions. Decision making is a critical part of operating any business. It is very difficult to always make the right decisions that will help the business to prosper. Often one is forced to choose between things that seem equal in every regard. How then, is one to know what is the proper action? Fortunately, the Higher Self is always available to give us guidance on such matters.

Edgar Cayce gave this advice to one businessman:

> **Depend more upon the intuitive forces from within and not harken so much to that of outside influences— but learn to listen to that still small voice from within, remembering as the lesson as was given, not in the storm, the lightning, nor in any of the loud noises as are made to attract man, but rather in the still small voice from within does the impelling influence come to life in an individual that gives for that which must be the basis of human endeavor; for without the ability to constantly hold before self the ideal as is attempted to be accomplished, man becomes one as adrift, pulled hither and yon by the various calls and cries of those who would give of this world's pleasure in fame, fortune, or whatnot.** (239-1)

Thus Cayce suggested that the guidance we are looking for comes from that "still small voice within," provided we are working toward some ideal. This voice is the Higher Self that speaks to us on some inner level. If our business endeavors are in line with our own personal spiritual ideal, then our Higher Self will give us any advice we need to be successful.

Meditation is perhaps the best way to contact the Higher Self. Other ways that may be more convenient in a business environment involve some of the tools of the trade. In decision making, the tools that operate under the principle of synchronicity can be readily applied. Some of these are tarot cards, the I Ching, and the Book of Runes. In using these techniques, a seemingly random event, such as the shuffling and dealing of cards, the tossing of coins, or the selection of a single stone from a bag, will provide answers to your questions. The Higher Self uses these tools by influencing the event, so that the outcome is exactly as it should be to provide the proper guidance.

Any of the tools of the trade can be used with great success in making decisions. However, there has been a recent adaptation of the Book of Changes, which tailors the I Ching specifically for business decisions. This book is called *The I Ching on Business & Decision Making* and is the creation of Guy Damian-Knight. He has taken the somewhat vague and difficult wording of the Book of Changes and specifically interpreted it in light of several types of business questions. The result is a system of divination that gives clear, easy to understand insights on business decisions of all types. For example, some business topics that are addressed are management, planning, creative judgement, advertising, marketing, investment, communications, start-up, and many more.

The Role of Education

Business and education are two topics that deserve to be treated together since they are so directly interrelated. The business community relies heavily on the educational systems to supply future employees with a knowledge of basic skills that will allow them to be creative participants in society. Education is the foundation upon which business is built. Increasingly, businesses are finding that the people they hire, although they finished school and may have attended college, are still not properly prepared to enter the high tech world of business.

A recent government report stated that the national high school graduation rate is 71.1%. This means that nearly three out of every ten children who enter school do not go on to graduate. These people who lack knowledge of basic skills are simply not qualified to perform in the business world. Although there are a few exceptions, many dropouts do not receive the same opportunities to contribute to society that educated people receive. As non-contributors they become burdens to the economic health of this nation that must care for them.

At the root of our decline in business influence as a nation, is the decline of the effectiveness of the education of our children. The children of the United States currently rank nineteenth among industrial nations in basic skills. Businesses are increasingly finding they need to re-educate their new employees in extensive training programs before they can become productive. Many "expert" opinions blame this on lack of funds and poor quality teachers. However, the real problem lies deeper than that.

Just as in business, the Law of Change is active in education. At one time our schools were adequate in preparing students for their lives ahead. There were only a limited number of opportunities and careers available, so only general basic skills in these areas were required. However, technological progress has been such that schools cannot keep up with all that must be taught. It seems there are always more subjects to be studied, as our scientific knowledge in many areas grows exponentially. Thus, schools are not able to provide students with an educational background that is suitable for everyone. This was once only true for high schools. But as the demand for higher skill levels on the job rose, more people found they needed to attend college to have a career. Now, even the colleges cannot keep up with the demands, and it is quickly becoming mandatory for a person to have a post-graduate degree before they can have a professional position in industry. As a result we are spending more of our years in school, and less time doing our life's work. Thus, there is an obvious lack of efficiency in our educational system if we must spend all our years between the ages of five to twenty-five just preparing for our life. At that point, the life of the average person is already more than a third over!

Our traditional form of education is no longer suitable for the new social environment in which we live. Since our schools cannot adequately teach all the subjects that every student will need to know, what they are choosing to teach is becoming increasingly irrelevant to what the student will eventually use when they graduate and get on with their life. The answer to this situation lies in taking education out of control of the government and putting it into the hands of business. Only professionals currently working in a field can truly know what is required learning for that career. They should be the ones who suggest what a student with an interest in that area should learn. Our children should be exposed to real working environments, with real problems to solve, at an early age. Businesses should be funded to provide classrooms where the students can spend part of their time learning related subjects and part of their time actually working with real professionals. These businesses could be all types, such as engineering firms, manufacturing plants, hospitals, publishing companies, retailers, restaurant companies, etc.. After some time in one of these businesses, the student can elect to stay and continue their education along those lines or move on to something else.

After experiencing many different types of careers first-hand, students will be better prepared to choose an occupation. Currently, most people enter a career not knowing what to expect. That is because we are currently forced to choose which college we will attend and which subjects we'll study while still in high school. High school life does not teach us enough about the adult world for us to make these decisions adequately.

Another advantage of placing education in the business world, is that students will be able to learn more quickly. Learning is much simpler when what is being taught is also being applied. In the October 1990 issue of *New Age Journal*, New York City teacher John Gatto stated, "When children are given whole lives instead of age-graded ones in cell blocks, they learn to read, write, and do arithmetic with ease if those things make sense in the life that unfolds around them." What our children need today, is less homework and less learning out of a book, and more learning in the school of life.

The Education of the Self

Anyone who has read up to this point in this book probably could predict that when it came to discussing education, I would stress the importance of giving our children education in spiritual teachings. Of course education about our Self, is the most important teaching we can receive. The Self includes the body, mind, and spirit, and none of these should be left out. The tool of meditation is a great way to have students get in touch with their own spirit. By learning to access this level of themselves they will learn how to discover their life's purpose and better decide who they should become.

Also, meditation can help develop one's ability to concentrate. Practicing meditation helps one to remove extraneous thoughts from their consciousness and access the higher levels of their mind. Martin Fiebert and Travis Mead, in a study published in 1981 in *Perceptual and Motor Skills*, found that students who meditate spend less time studying, without dropping in academic performance. They also found that meditating just before studying or taking an exam improves one's performance.

Traditionally, American culture has put great emphasis on the separation of church and state. The spirit is a taboo subject in our classrooms. The government controlled schools are mandated not to discuss such things because of the controversy it would cause. This controversy is due to the religious fanaticism that has been so prevalent in our society. Most people, even if they don't currently attend church, believe in some religious doctrine, and are completely terrified of other religions which conflict with their own. People are comfortable with what they believe, and they resist any new or different idea that may shake their religious foundation. Thus, in a country with many different religions, the government takes the safe way out by leaving spiritual education up to the churches.

Unfortunately, religions as they exist today are antiquated and are holding back the spiritual development of humanity. The teachings that are preached in churches today are thousands of years old. That was a different age then, and humanity was at a different level of development. We simply were not yet ready to integrate all of the great spiritual truths of our existence. Thus, religions tried to make it simple for us by personifying the image of God and creating physical places in our mind known as heaven and hell. These teachings led us to believe in our separateness from God instead of believing of ourselves as cells in the body and mind of God. The truth is we are all God and we create our own heaven and hell.

In this new age, humanity is beginning to evolve at a greatly accelerated rate. As this age evolves, spiritual things are becoming more important to us. People are increasingly asking, "Is this all there is, or am I something more than this that will continue when this life is over?" This is a sign that we as spirit beings are beginning to awaken to our own true nature.

The time is soon coming when spiritual growth will be foremost on everyone's mind. Thus, the need is already here to begin incorporating the teachings of this age into every child's learning. All of the topics and techniques that I have discussed in this book are important fundamentals. This list includes meditation, dreams, obtaining guidance, healing, the oneness of the universe, and most importantly the nature and destiny of humans as evolving god beings. With this background a student can learn to become their own teacher, as they discover their inner self and connect with the universal source of all knowledge.

Prayer for Business and Career Success

Dear Father, grant us all we need to properly carry out our purpose on this planet. Help us to recognize our talents and abilities, and to use these according to your will. Help us to find the highest spiritual ideal within ourselves and always to work in harmony with it. Help us to freely accept and welcome the changes in our lives that are necessary for our growth. Help us to work together and in harmony with one another, making the world more peaceful through mutual cooperation. As one prospers may we all prosper, Lord. In these and all things we ask of thee, may your will be done. Amen.

Meditation for a Spiritual Ideal

This meditation will guide you to find the highest purpose in your life. You will find the work that you could do that would bring the most joy and fulfillment to your life.

Close your eyes and relax your body. Ask yourself this question: "What am I here to do?" Pause a few seconds, and repeat the question. Continue to repeat the question for as long as you like, and then allow your mind to become quiet.

Free yourself of all doubts and all thoughts of circumstances in your life that make you uncomfortable. Imagine that you are free from all ties. You are on your own now in the quiet recesses of your mind. Suddenly you begin to have thoughts or see a picture in your mind like you were dreaming. What are you doing? Are you happy? Are you sad? Continue to allow these impressions to enter your mind. Focus on being happy. What could you possibly do that would make you the happiest you've ever been?

Continue this meditation as long as you like. You are in touch with your Higher Self now. It's that easy. It's always been that easy to find your inner guidance. Know that your Higher Self loves you. It does not judge you. It only wants you to find the most fulfillment you can. Bless yourself. Say to yourself, "I love myself for who I am." Repeat this over and over.

You are divine, you know. You are a piece of God, and you may do whatever you choose according to your highest good and the good of others. Stay with your Higher Self as long as you like. Feel loved. Feel whole. Know that when you return to your normal state of consciousness you can always call on your Higher Self whenever you like. Have conversations with it. Talk to it. After all it's you.

AFTERWORD

In this book I have attempted to convey the practical application of many of the spiritual teachings that one may discover. I have focussed the purpose of this application on improving the society and culture in which we live. What I have presented is only a small beginning and I have only barely scratched the surface of all that one may discover on the many spiritual paths. I hope this book has inspired all of those who have read it to learn more about their inner self and to begin to recognize spiritual growth in all that they experience. I also sincerely hope that we as part of humanity can see our problems in a new light and propose solutions which facilitate our group spiritual development. May God bless us all in this endeavor.

APPENDIX

References

The following of a list of the resource materials that I used for this book. These books and tapes have been most helpful in my spiritual growth and I highly recommend them for everyone.

Books:

The Aquarian Gospel of Jesus the Christ, by Levi. DeVorss and Company, Marina del Rey, CA 90294-0550, 1964.
 The channeled account of the life and teachings of Jesus the Christ.

Astrology and the Edgar Cayce Readings, by Margaret H. Gammon. A.R.E. Press, Virginia Beach, VA, 1967.
 A unique introduction to astrology.

Autobiography of a Yogi, by Paramahansa Yogananda. Self Realization Fellowship, 3880 San Rafael Avenue, Los Angeles, CA 90065, 1974.
 How one man mastered the eastern techniques of enlightenment and brought them to the West.

A Commentary on the Book of Revelation, Based on a Study of Twenty-Four Psychic Discourses by Edgar Cayce. A.R.E. Press, Virginia Beach, VA, 1945.
 A complete and thorough interpretation of the least understood and perhaps most important book of the Bible.

Cheiro's Palmistry for All, by Cheiro. Prentice Hall Press, One Gulf and Western Plaza, New York, NY 10023, 1964.
 Just one of the many introductory books currently available on palmistry.

IT'S TIME TO MAKE IT HAPPEN ON EARTH

A Complete Guide to the Tarot, by Eden Gray. Bantam Books, 666 Fifth Avenue, New York, NY 10103, 1970.
  My favorite book on how to read tarot cards.

Creating Money: Keys to Abundance, by Sanaya Roman and Duane Packer. HJ Kramer Inc., P.O. Box 1082, Tiburon, CA 94920, 1988.
  A channeled book on how to get what you need to fulfill your life's work.

Dancing in the Light, by Shirley Maclaine. Bantam Books, 666 Fifth Avenue, New York, NY 10103, 1985.
  Personal accounts of Shirley's spiritual quest after the period of *Out on a Limb.*

Edgar Cayce Encyclopedia of Healing, by Reba Ann Karp. Warner Books, Inc., 666 Fifth Avenue, New York, NY 10103, 1986.
  Cayce's diagnoses and treatments for 190 ailments.

Edgar Cayce on Reincarnation, by Noel Langley. Warner Books, Inc., 1967.
  The Cayce readings on the subject of reincarnation and also the account of Justinian and Theodora.

Edgar Cayce's Story of Jesus, by Jeffrey Furst. Berkley Publishing Group, 200 Madison Avenue, New York, NY 10016, 1968.
  Cayce's account of the past lives of Jesus.

Edgar Cayce's Story of Karma, by Mary Ann Woodward. Berkley Publishing Group, 1971.
  The Cayce readings on the Law of Karma.

50 Simple Things You Can Do To Save The Earth, by the Earthworks Group, Box 25, 1400 Shattuck Avenue, Berkeley, CA 94709.
  The Earth can be saved if we act now. Find out what you can do as an individual.

God's Other Door, by Hugh Lynn Cayce. A.R.E. Press, Virginia Beach, VA, 1958.
  Edgar Cayce's description of the spirit planes and spirit communication.

The Gulf Breeze Sightings, by Ed and Frances Walters. William Morrow and Company, Inc., 105 Madison Avenue, New York, NY 10016, 1990.
  The written accounts and color photographs of one couple's UFO experience.

Going Within: A Guide for Inner Transformation, by Shirley Maclaine. Bantam Books, New York, NY, 1989.
> Shirley gives techniques for enlightenment in her normally entertaining style.

The I Ching on Business and Decision Making, by Guy Damian-Knight. Destiny Books, One Park Street, Rochester, Vermont 05767, 1986.
> An easy tool for intuitive business decisions.

The Inner Power of Silence: A Universal Way of Meditation, by Mark Thurston. Inner Vision Publishing Company, Box 1117 Seapines Station, Virginia Beach, VA 23451, 1986.
> The hows and whys of meditation.

The Journey Within: Past-Life Regression and Channeling, by Henry Leo Bolduc. Inner Vision Publishing Company, Virginia Beach, VA, 1988.
> Henry Boluc's personal account of his discovery of past life hypnotic regression and channeling.

Karmic Tarot, by William C. Lammey. Newcastle Publishing Company, Inc., P.O. Box 7589, Van Nuys, CA 91409, 1988.
> A unique system of tarot card reading based upon knowledge of the planes of self.

Keys to Health—The Promise and Challenge of Holism, by Eric Mein, M.D.. Harper and Row, Publishers, Inc., 10 East 53rd Street, New York, NY 10022, 1989.
> The Edgar Cayce approach to holistic healing.

Linda Goodman's Star Signs, by Linda Goodman. St. Martin's Press, 175 Fifth Avenue, New York, NY 10010, 1987.
> A book that gives practical applications of the tools of the trade.

Meditation: Gateway to Light, by Elsie Sechrist. A.R.E. Press, Virginia Beach, VA, 1972.
> The Edgar Cayce readings on meditation.

The Mystical Qabala, by Dion Fortune. Samuel Weiser, Inc., Box 612, York Beach, ME 03910, 1984.
> An advanced text on the nature of reality.

Mysteries of the Unknown, series by Time-Life Books, Alexandria, VA, 1989-.
> A wonderfully written and lavishly illustrated book series which gives an introduction to everything metaphysical.

The Newcastle Guide to Healing with Crystals, by Jonathan Pawlik and Pamela Chase. Newcastle Publishing Company, Inc., Van Nuys, CA, 1988.
> Healing with life force energy and how to magnify it with crystals.

Out on a Limb, by Shirley Maclaine. Bantam Books, New York, NY, 1983.
> The modern classic of the New Age.

Prescription for Nutritional Healing, by James F. Balch, M.D. and Phyllis A. Balch, C.N.C.. Avery Publishing Group, Inc., Garden City Park, NY, 1990.
> An indispensible health reference book of common ailments and alternative treatments.

The Secret Government—The Origin, Identity, and Purpose of MJ-12, by Milton William Cooper. Cosmic Awareness Communications, P.O. Box 115, Olympia, WA 98507, 1989.
> Also known as "The William Cooper Papers," this article explains much of the history of our government's involvement with aliens.

Seed Money in Action, by Dr. Jon Speller. Morning Star Press, P.O. Box 1095, Grand Central Station, New York, NY 10163, 1989.
> A small booklet on prosperity through the power of faith.

Self-Hypnosis: Creating Your Own Destiny, by Henry Leo Bolduc. A.R.E. Press, Virginia Beach, VA, 1985.
> How to make your own self-hypnosis cassette tapes.

Audio Tapes:

1989 World Prophecy, by Paul Solomon. The Fellowship of the Inner Light, 620 14th Street, Virginia Beach, VA 23451.

One of many recorded channeling sessions from Paul Solomon which comment on the evolution of humanity.

Edgar Cayce—Awaken Your Psychic Powers, by Mark Thurston. Audio Renaissance Tapes, Inc., 9110 Sunset Blvd., Suite 240, Los Angeles, CA 90069, 1987.

Edgar Cayce—Channeling Your Higher Self. Audio Renaissance Tapes, Inc., 1988.

Edgar Cayce—Meditation, by Mark Thurston. Audio Renaissance Tapes, Inc., 1988.

Edgar Cayce—Reincarnation and Past Lives, by Mark Thurston. Audio Renaissance Tapes, Inc., 1988.

Edgar Cayce—Understanding Your Dreams. Audio Renaissance Tapes, Inc., 1987.

All of the Audio Renaissance cassette tapes are great sources of information for those who prefer to listen than read.

Hopi Prophecies and Predictions for the New Age, by Thomas Banyacya. A recorded lecture available from the A.R.E., Virginia Beach, VA.

The view of our world from the perspective of the Hopi Indians.

Channeling Your Higher Self, by David J. Condon. Published by Transformation Publishing, Wayne, NJ.

A self-hypnosis tape designed to condition your mind to easily channel your Higher Self for guidance.

Remembering Your Past Lives, by David J. Condon. Published by Transformation Publishing, Wayne, NJ.

A self-hypnosis past life regression that leads you back to the memories of past lives.

Periodicals:

Connecting Link. 4025 Broadmoor S.E., P.O. Box 891, Grand Rapids, MI 49518. (616) 949-7894

Spirit Speaks: Insight Through Channeling. P.O. Box 84304, Los Angeles, CA 90049. (800) 356-9104

Both magazines publish current channeled information.

Associations and Organizations

The Association for Research and Enlightenment, P.O. Box 595, Virginia Beach, Virginia 23451.

The Association for Research and Enlightenment (A.R.E.) is a membership organization dedicated to continuing the work of Edgar Cayce and making the readings available to the general public. The A.R.E. publishes books, a magazine, and several newsletters. It sponsors local study groups, a Prison Outreach program, a youth camp, and many lectures and symposiums throughout the country. The Edgar Cayce readings are housed in the A.R.E. library and are available on loan to members by mail. This space is too limited to adequately describe all of their activities, but you can write them for a free brochure.

The Aquarian Church of Universal Service, Inc., P.O. Box 12072, Portland, Oregon 97212.

The Aquarian Church is an organization that explores and applies the teachings of the source that is called Cosmic Awareness, or the Universal Consciousness. This organization publishes handbooks, pamphlets and home study courses, as well as provides spiritual development classes given throughout the country.

Cosmic Awareness Communications, P.O. Box 115, Olympia, Washington 98507.

Cosmic Awareness Communications (CAC) publishes a newsletter every three weeks containing the latest Cosmic Awareness readings based upon questions received from members. These newsletters contain interesting insights on all subjects including the most current news items.

The National Arbor Day Foundation, 100 Arbor Ave., Nebraska City, NE 68410.

This organization plants trees to help save our planet.

The Nature Conservancy, 1815 North Lynn Street, Arlington, VA 22209. (703) 841-5300.

An organization which buys up vast acres of unspoiled land and maintains them as wildlife preserves.

Food Grade Hydrogen Peroxide is available from:
Vital Health Products Ltd.
PO Box 164, Muskego, WI 53150
(414) 422-0522

Acknowledgments

I wish to thank the following sources for allowing me to quote from their books or tapes:

The Edgar Cayce readings and Kevin Ryerson quotes used with permission of the Edgar Cayce Foundation, P.O. Box 595, Virginia Beach, VA 23451.

The Paul Solomon readings used with permission of Paul Solomon Foundation, 620 14th Street, Virginia Beach, VA 23451.

Excerpts from *You Can Heal Your Life* used with permission of Louise L. Hay, Hay House, Inc.

Excerpts from *The Journey Within* used with permission of Henry Leo Bolduc, P.O. Box 88, Independence, VA 24348.

Cosmic Awareness readings used with permission of Cosmic Awareness Communications, P.O. Box 115, Olympia, WA 98507.

Excerpts from *Creating Money: Keys to Abundance* used with permission of HJ Kramer, Inc., P.O. Box 1082, Tiburon, CA 94920. All rights reserved.

GLOSSARY

Ages — twelve periods of 2160 years each associated with a sign of the zodiac.

Akashic Records — the records of life, every thought, every action, contained in the Universal Mind.

Aquarian Age — the current new age of social awareness and humanitarian concerns.

Astrology — the study of the correspondences between human experience and celestial activity.

Aura — the soul energy surrounding the body usually consisting of one or more colors that are visible to some people who possess a high level of awareness.

Chakras — the energy vortices connecting the higher bodies to the physical, of which there are seven primary ones.

Channeling — the act of receiving and transmitting information from spiritual realms.

Conscious Mind — the ego self. That portion of the mind that embodies the personality of an individual, and is the point of focus for the soul's expression in the earth plane.

Cosmic Awareness — that connection with the Universal Mind that expresses itself through those able to raise their consciousness to its level of vibration.

Cosmic Laws — those fixed and unchanging concepts that define all of creation.

Entity — spirit energy that possesses individuality.

Esoteric — that which is generally hidden from the public.

Exoteric — that which is judged suitable for public consumption.

Grace — divine love and protection bestowed upon those who serve others.

Higher Self — that part of human consciousness that is perpetually in harmony with the Divine will and seeks to guide the individual on its quest for soul growth.

Higher Self Channeling — the act of raising one's conscious mind to the level of the Higher Self while maintaining a point of physical grounding, thereby retaining the ability to speak and transmit messages from one's Higher Self.

I Ching — a method of divination where one is guided to read a section in the *Book of Changes* after tossing coins or yarrow sticks.

Karma — subconscious memory of previous deeds that indicate the need for additional experiences to balance one's actions and complete their lessons.

Meditation — the process of releasing everyday concerns and obtaining a deep level of relaxation while maintaining conscious awareness. It is a tool that may be used for personal reflection and greater understanding of one's purpose.

Mediumship — the act of allowing an entity in the spirit plane to temporarily occupy one's body, usually for the purpose of communicating with someone in the physical plane.

Metaphysics — the branch of philosophy concerning the fundamental nature of reality including that which may not always conform to present scientific definitions.

Natal Chart — an astrological description of the planetary positions in the sky at the moment of birth as viewed from the location of birth. Interpretation of this information describes the basic characteristics and tendencies of the individual throughout life.

Numerology — the study of the influence of numbers on human experience.

Palmistry — the study of the lines and characteristics of the hand and palm and their correlation with human experience.

Possession — the state of being wherein a spiritual entity has seized control of another's physical body against the will of the owner.

Prana (Chi) — that life force energy contained in all of creation.

Prayer — the act of requesting assistance from one's Higher Self and the divine realms and the seeking of greater attunement to same.

Progressed Chart — an astrological description of the present or future planetary positions relative to one's natal chart. Interpretation of this information reveals the timing and nature of likely experiences and lessons.

Reincarnation — the process of entering into multiple earthly lifetimes to increase one's understanding of themselves and Cosmic Law.

Soul — all portions of oneself that survive physical death and give life to form.

Subconscious Mind — that portion of the human consciousness that retains memory of all life experience both during physical incarnations and between.

Superconscious Mind — see Higher Self.

Synchronicity — the meaningful coincidence of multiple experiences usually occurring close in time to one another for the purpose of communicating a message from the Higher Self.

Tarot — a method of divination using a deck of 78 cards depicting a language of symbols and color.

Universal Mind — the collective consciousness of all of creation and that which is without limitation in wisdom and knowledge.

Yoga — a Hindu discipline for attunement to the Higher realms.-

Audio Cassettes by David J. Condon

It's Time to Make It Happen on Earth—Meditations and Prayers

A companion to the book, this tape contains all the meditations and prayers found at the end of each chapter. Recorded in his own voice, David leads the listener onto peaceful, restful journeys that not only transform the individual, but also help to heal society and the planet. The tape also features original music by the author as accompaniment.

Channeling Your Higher Self—With Self Hypnosis and Guided Imagery

Meet your Higher Self through this guided visualization experience. You will learn David's unique nine step technique for channeling your Higher Self to obtain guidance for yourself and others. Repeated use of this tape conditions your mind to make contacting your Higher Self an easy and natural process. Through this contact your intuition and sense of life purpose become increasingly clear.

Remembering Your Past Lives—Past Life Regression

Journey deep into your subconscious to uncover memories of past lifetimes. You will travel with your Higher Self into the bodies of former lifetimes and experience the sensation of being there again. This tape is a completely safe self-hypnotic induction that allows you to remain in control of your experience. You may use the tape to research past lives that are connected to your present attitudes and emotions, bringing about self transformation and healing.

Order Form

Your Name _____

Address _____

City _____ State _____ Zip _____

Please provide your telephone number in case we have any questions about your order:

Home (_____) _____ Work (_____) _____

	UNIT PRICE	QTY.	TOTAL PRICE
It's Time to Make It Happen on Earth (Book)	$ 9.95		
It's Time to Make It Happen on Earth (Audio Cassette of Meditations and Prayers)	$ 9.95		
Channeling Your Higher Self (Audio Cassette)	$ 9.95		
Remembering Your Past Lives (Audio Cassette)	$ 9.95		
* New Jersey residents include 6% ($ .60 per item) sales tax.	Subtotal		
	*Sales Tax		
Shipping Charges: $ 2.00 for first item plus $ .50 for each additional item.	Shipping		
	TOTAL		

Payment enclosed: ☐ Check ☐ Money Order

Please charge my: ☐ Visa ☐ Master Card

Credit Card No. _____ Expiration Date _____

Signature as on card _____

Please make checks payable to **Transformation Publishing.** Canadian and foreign orders make checks payable in U.S. funds and please add $ 2.00 per order for additional postage.

Telephone orders call: **1-800-453-0499**